welcome to Dragon Talk

welcome to Dragon Talk

INSPIRING CONVERSATIONS ABOUT DUNGEONS & DRAGONS AND THE PEOPLE WHO LOVE TO PLAY IT

Shelly Mazzanoble and Greg Tito

Cohosts of the Official D&D Podcast

UNIVERSITY OF IOWA PRESS • IOWA CITY

University of Iowa Press, Iowa City 52242

Copyright © 2022 by Shelly Mazzanoble and Greg Tito

uipress.uiowa.edu

Printed in the United States of America

Design by April Leidig

Printed on acid-free paper

Library of Congress Cataloging-in-Publication Data
Names: Mazzanoble, Shelly, 1972– author, interviewer. |
    Tito, Greg, 1978– author, interviewer.
Title: Welcome to Dragon Talk: Inspiring Conversations about
    Dungeons & Dragons and the People Who Love to Play It /
    by Shelly Mazzanoble and Greg Tito.
Description: Iowa City: University of Iowa Press, 2022.
Identifiers: LCCN 2022003433 (print) | LCCN 2022003434 (ebook) |
    ISBN 9781609388591 (paperback) | ISBN 9781609388607 (ebook)
Subjects: LCSH: Dungeons & Dragons (Game) | Fantasy gamers—
    Interviews.
Classification: LCC GV1469.62.D84 M43 2022 (print) |
    LCC GV1469.62.D84 (ebook) | DDC 793.93—dc23/eng/20220321
LC record available at https://lccn.loc.gov/2022003433
LC ebook record available at https://lccn.loc.gov/2022003434

This book is dedicated to everyone who ever convinced
a friend or family member to play D&D with them. We lift you up!

For my daughters, Edna and Fiona, future Dungeon Masters. (G. T.)

For Quinn, a.k.a. Chunky Cheese, the wizard who casts spells
out of his butt and who will always be my hero. (S. M.)

CONTENTS

welcome to Dragon Talk

What Is D&D?

I've been asked this question a thousand times.

Dungeons & Dragons (D&D) is a tabletop roleplaying game (RPG) where players make decisions based on how their fantasy character would act when presented with a challenge or adversary by the player acting as the Dungeon Master.

Maybe I didn't explain that quite right.

Dragon Talk, the podcast Shelly and I cohost and the subject of the book you're reading, is about making sure everyone knows that this game is for all types of people. Describing D&D in just a sentence doesn't really encompass the true majesty of the game. Shelly may have written a bit of marketing copy that gives more context:

> *Dungeons & Dragons* is a cooperative storytelling game driven by the limitless possibilities of your imagination. Silly moments spawn inside jokes; overcoming challenges leaves treasured memories—whether in the heat of battle, embroiled in social intrigue, or solving clever puzzles, your adventuring party has your back. D&D brings people together and forges new friendships.

That's better, but even that doesn't really explain the typical roles, what a wizard is, or how a paladin feels different than a fighter. One of the first things you do before playing D&D is create a character. Players take on archetypes like the dashing rogue, the stern holy warrior, the elven sorceress, or any variation they imagine and try to complete the Dungeon Master's storyline by improvising with fellow players. For players who love the strategy side of playing games, there's also a tactical system in play that allows D&D to simulate cinematic battles and force risky decisions that could result in success or failure based on the roll of a die. Players can go as deep into that as they want, or as the story serves, at any particular moment. There are sessions that don't involve rolling any dice at all and might feel more like improv theater, while a climactic confrontation against the evil villain might be a session that's nothing but swings of the sword or slings of the spell and your hands are calloused from rolling so many dice.

That may not make sense yet. You have to play D&D to realize you may be able to technically describe it with a pithy sentence but that's just scratching at the surface. The experience of playing D&D can go really deep. It can also be pretty shallow, with nothing but potty humor and cheese dust on your hands.

D&D is like building a cathedral—in your mind! Playing D&D uses so many disciplines, so many different parts of the brain. It's a framework for storytelling. It's a strategy game of life. It's a simulation asking, "What if?" It's theater. It's cinema. It's a video game. *Dungeons & Dragons* teaches empathy, communication, arithmetic, logic, tactics, soft skills, project management. It asks you to prioritize cooperation, celebrate your cohorts, and resolve conflict efficiently. Playing D&D can feel as elegant as a ballet, as silly as a farting pig, and as tense as a drive-in horror film. You build friendships playing D&D that can last a lifetime, and there's nothing sweeter than a family slaying the dragon together.

I've been asked "What is D&D?" so many times from people at random corporate events, at the dentist, or while waiting for my kids after school when someone asks what the ampersand on my T-shirt means.

It always goes better when I use an example. "Say you are walking through the woods, and I say 'Oh no! A goblin runs out snarling and brandishing a rusty sword. What do you do?'" Then the person would invariably be like, "Uhhh." And I'd say, "You want to shoot an arrow at it, maybe, but then you don't know if you are going to hit the goblin, he's a hundred feet away, so roll this d20." I always have a twenty-sided die with me for exactly these situations!

I roll the die, and if it's above a ten, I'll say, "Yay, you hit it! Congratulations! That's D&D."

I usually win my Persuasion check there, but not always.[1] It doesn't feel

---

1. Greg: In D&D, a Persuasion (Charisma) check is something a DM will call for a player to make if they are trying to convince someone of something or if you are

right with me talking to myself. I'm like a DM trying to run a conversation between two non-player characters (NPCs) here![2]

Wait, I have an idea. Maybe Shelly's tabaxi sorcerer, Drunky Two-Shoes, is available for a quick session. Since about 2020, on the *Dragon Talk* podcast, we've been closing out the episode with a five-minute D&D session. Shelly plays Drunky Two-Shoes; I'm the DM and also Daryl Two-Shoes, Drunky's littermate. Did I mention that tabaxis are cat people?

> **Greg:** Okay, Drunky. You are in a deserted alley in the city of Waterdeep. You think your brother is hiding out here in the alley, trying to stay away from the Xanathar's guild enforcers he stole that beer from. What do you do?
>
> **Shelly:** Tell Daryl he better share that beer with me when I find him. I'm going to walk down this alley and look for him.
>
> **Greg:** Are you going to move any of the crates or garbage around, or are you standing still looking and listening?
>
> **Shelly:** I'm going to topple over the garbage cans and throw those crates against the walls in hopes that if bad guys are lurking around here, they'll be scared and run away.
>
> **Greg:** Okay, so roll me an Investigation check.
>
> **Shelly:** I rolled an eight, but with my Investigation bonus it's an eleven.
>
> **Greg:** All right. You spend a few minutes moving around all the boxes and crates, loudly of course, which scares a small rat that scurries away, and underneath one pile of broken wood, you realize the ground is soaked with liquid.
>
> **Shelly:** Is it clumping???
>
> **Greg:** No, it's not kitty litter. (*laughs*) But it does smell really good to your senses!
>
> **Shelly:** Okay, I stick my paw in the liquid and lick it. Does it taste like beer by chance?

---

attempting to make yourself understood. The player rolls a twenty-sided die, adds any bonuses if their character is good with words, and hopefully the result is high enough to convince the town guard to let you through.

2. Greg: NPCs are run by the Dungeon Master. They move the story forward and the DM can use them to give information or plot hooks that the players could pursue. Some DMs use distinct voices or accents for each of their NPCs. All of Shelly's sound like C-3PO.

Greg: It does. And as you are crouched down licking the beer off the ground, you hear a voice behind you say, "Oi! We got your boy right here, kitty!" You see three burly humans holding a limp furry form in front of them. What do you do?

Shelly: I cast *fog cloud*! But by accident because they startled me.

Greg: Wait, is that because you sharted?

Shelly: It's dark here. You'll never know. Also Drunky's not wearing pants. (*laughs*)

Greg: Okay then, roll for initiative!

From there Shelly and I take turns describing our actions and use the D&D rules to resolve the effects of swinging a longsword or casting *magic missile*. The story is built over the session, a fixed time of play, like three hours each Wednesday, and those sessions combined form a campaign that can last a few months, years, or even decades.

Dungeons & Dragons has a long history, and it has changed, morphed, and had major hiccups in its development from the different teams making it over the four decades it has been around. The current D&D team at Wizards of the Coast, of which Shelly and I are a part, consider themselves the stewards of this important tradition. D&D doesn't really belong to any one company or entity but to the fans who play and love it. The D&D team may publish adventures and rules, but it's all designed to inspire because it is the fans who actually make this game great.

That's been the thesis statement of *Dragon Talk* from the beginning: to lift up the voices of the community and shine a spotlight on storytelling techniques and occasional critiques of *Dungeons & Dragons*. The bulk of this book is composed of essays written by Shelly or me, shedding even more light on the compelling stories and important aspects of the D&D community through the lens of various interviews we've conducted over the years.

To understand all that nuance, it's helpful to know the backstory—both the history of *Dungeons & Dragons* and the history of the *Dragon Talk* podcast. Hardcore fans may be aware of some of the events described in the next section, but some of the later stuff on the inner workings of the D&D brand since about 2011 has never been discussed publicly. We try to show how the fans who play D&D have just as much (if not more) of an impact on the game throughout its history. We also weave in our own personal experiences—

our own "origin stories" with D&D that we often ask podcast guests to describe—placing us in the history of the game, aspects of which come up a lot in the following essays.

Take a journey with Shelly and me as we walk you through . . .

The History of D&D and the Community around It (Greg)

. . . the story so far.

Dungeons & Dragons was first published in 1974 by Gary E. Gygax and Dave Arneson. It was an evolution of the wargames they played involving armies of miniature figurines marching over homemade terrain. They would play in hobby shops, bookstores, or anywhere there was a big enough room. For larger gatherings, gamers would set up wide tables in small event spaces like the Horticultural Hall in Lake Geneva, Wisconsin, where Gygax lived with his family. Imagine rows of small pewter carvings of knights in shining armor meticulously painted to match medieval heraldry with crude scenery such as a popsicle stick with cotton balls glued to it and spray-painted green to represent the trees, and you wouldn't be too far off.

D&D's biggest innovation was that instead of a competitive game with players controlling military units fighting against each other, players took on the roles of individual fantasy archetypes, like warriors, magic users, and martially minded clerics, and worked together to solve the challenges the Dungeon Master would throw at them. The first D&D games were focused on progressing through a branching dungeon full of rooms with various monsters to kill and/or treasure to plunder. That gameplay boiled down to basically this: get treasure and bring it back to town, sell it, collect experience points, get stronger, and go deeper in the dungeon to kill harder baddies like beholders, mind flayers, and the occasional adult red dragon with fiery breath. Collect *their* treasure. Lather, rinse, repeat.

The first D&D game had a print run of about a thousand copies, and the legend goes that Gygax drove around to local Wisconsin college campuses, crashed wargaming club meetings, and sold them the D&D rulebooks for ten bucks a pop out of the trunk of his car. The polyhedral dice needed to play were a few bucks more. Because of this ingenious marketing campaign, or maybe just because the rules he was peddling were actually pretty enticing, *Dungeons & Dragons* caught on with enough wargamers who were looking for something different. That first print run of 1,000 sold out within a year, and the second 1,000 sold out in seven months. With that, D&D began to make money.

This is also when the community around the game first coalesced. Like D&D itself, it grew out of the wargaming community. Gygax and Arneson, along with a couple hundred other gamers, met at the second Gen Con in 1969,[3] and they continued to correspond and debate with each other as they worked on writing rules. You see, those (shall we say) spirited discussions in a small part of the wargaming community were exactly what created *Dungeons & Dragons* in the first place, and that *new* D&D community continued to foster the growth of early D&D roleplaying by organizing events and publishing zines and other self-printed supplements across the Midwest. Some of the individuals who were important in that community were hired to create official D&D material or started gaming companies of their own, like Judges Guild in Illinois and Games Workshop Group in England. The community around D&D grew.

While that sounds all hunky-dory, it's important to realize this nascent community was composed of misfits who loved to strategize how their wizard would defeat a vile lich, but they didn't always know how to fight real evil within their own ranks. Many gamers of that era had yet to understand how systemic racism or misogyny could manifest in their hobby, a young Greg Tito included (more on that in the essays that follow). Most D&D community members were white men, and while some of them surely witnessed bigotry at their gaming tables and did nothing to prevent it, others didn't realize how some of their behaviors might affect those who were not white men.

The new community of D&D players was on the edge of culture, similar to the punk movement in music. They were forging a niche for themselves and their tastes away from the mainstream. But like the punk scene, it was really difficult to be in that culture in the late 1970s if you weren't a white dude. Women and those from marginalized groups like LGBTQIA+ and people of color were certainly all there playing D&D, but a lot of them were pushed out

---

3. Greg: This event was officially called the Lake Geneva Wargaming Convention, named after its location in Lake Geneva, Wisconsin. But gamers referred to it as the Geneva Convention, which was a reference to treaties governing the rules of international warfare signed after World War II. Get it? Rules of war? Wargaming convention? Anyway, the nickname stuck and was eventually shortened to just Gen Con. Gamers love a good pun, and this won't be the first you read in this book!

of the community, erased from most of the collective memories or memoirs written about the time. Gatekeeping, intentional and unintentional, kept these groups feeling targeted in the D&D community. The bigoted behavior from some members of that community made playing D&D unpalatable for many; it was healthier to walk away than constantly fight misogyny, mistreatment, or worse in what is supposed to be leisure time. I don't believe the majority of the new leaders of this community chose to create the hostile atmosphere felt by some marginalized groups in the early D&D community, but they certainly didn't take enough specific actions to address it.

Perhaps some of the gatekeeping and negative behaviors toward women were reinforced by the way pulp science fiction and fantasy stories were illustrated in the 1950s and 1960s, with chainmail bikinis and other nonsense. D&D illustrations in the 1970s were no different, with women usually depicted as scantily clad victims (if at all). And if you can point me to an illustration of a Black person (who isn't a drow) in an early D&D book, I'd love to see it.

Don't worry, we'll get back to this point later. Things do get better! Unfortunately, the company that published D&D had other, more existential demons to battle before it would take on bigotry.

Before publishing D&D in 1974, Gygax started a company and called it Tactical Studies Rules (TSR). Once D&D sold enough copies to start earning profits, TSR hired more game designers to create new content and continue revising the rules. They published a new version of the game in 1978 and called it *Advanced Dungeons & Dragons* (AD&D) while keeping a more streamlined game available for newbies on the shelves as basic. This is when D&D really took off and sparked imaginations around the world in the late 1970s. D&D's popularity spread into the mainstream in the early 1980s—you may have seen the D&D cartoon on Saturday mornings or remember the early scene in Steven Spielberg's movie *E.T.* where Elliot's older brother is playing with the neighborhood kids.

Then the backlash came, and it came down hard. Many people cite the Tom Hanks TV movie *Mazes & Monsters* in 1982 as demonizing roleplaying games enough to scare parents away from letting their kids play. I honestly think D&D just got caught up in the conservative Christian fearmongering of the Reagan era that led to banning heavy metal music, burning books, and basically acting all snooty toward anything that encouraged rational thought in the young. On the surface, skimming through *Monstrous Manual* or *Dragon* magazine would be pretty terrifying for the churchgoing crowd because it provides statistics for, you know, the *actual* devil.[4] But most of their arguments fell apart when one realized that D&D players embodied the heroes contending against those evil foes, and you can't tell a good story without having villains. Seriously, look at the famous Jack Chick tract about D&D, "Dark Dungeons."[5] It willfully misrepresents basically everything about the game to make it seem as horrifying as possible. Plus, if you believe that someone can actually cast magic mind-control spells, maybe the problem is your own stupidity, and not the fantasy gaming and fiction your precious child is inspired by.

If you can tell I'm still pissed at my Catholic mom for not letting me make friends with kids who played D&D in the 1980s then, congratulations, you can see more clearly than she could.

Gary Gygax was ousted as the leader of TSR in 1985 while he was busy focusing on the D&D cartoon and other potential entertainment deals, all of which fell apart after the backlash. Other historians like Jon Peterson have documented those events meticulously, but the short version is the small board of directors for TSR didn't appreciate how Gygax wrested control from them in early 1985, and they engineered a way to take a controlling interest in the company built on his work.[6] Gygax was forced to resign as president, but the company was still open to him working as an employee. Rather than let nongamers control his life's work, he left the company entirely in 1986 after he lost the legal battle to regain control.

With Gygax gone, TSR published the second edition of AD&D in 1989 with Dave "Zeb" Cook as lead designer. Even though the words "second edition" were on the cover, it's important to realize it was more like a whole new line of products, a new series of rulebooks and adventures that were a complete reboot of the rules TSR published under Gygax. Most (if not all) of the material published before was rendered obsolete unless one converted the underlying math to fit the new system. The second edition also filed off the serial numbers of a lot of the crap that seemed to piss off the Christian conservatives. Maybe they thought if they just called devils "baatezu" and demons "tanar'ri,"

4. Greg: TSR published a monthly magazine that included D&D discussion, supplementary rules, and adventures. It was a staple in the community at the time.

5. Greg: You can find the tract here: https://www.chick.com/products/tract?stk=0046.

6. Greg: Check out Jon Peterson's book *Game Wizards: The Epic Battle for Dungeons & Dragons* (MIT Press, 2021) for a more detailed account of this event.

no one would be mad at them anymore. That didn't work exactly as predicted, and after a short boom following the release of second edition, profits waned in the 1990s. TSR published a lot of books during this period, including some of the most well-loved campaign settings, like *Dark Sun*, *Planescape*, and *Ravenloft*. Some publishing snafus, including big bets on a dice game and twelve (!) novels that didn't sell that well from 1996 to 1997, reduced TSR's cash reserves and put the company $30 million in debt.

Because of all that, Wizards of the Coast bought TSR in 1997, as it was going insolvent. Formed in 1990 to publish roleplaying games in the Seattle area, Wizards had been printing money in the form of Magic cards since 1993. The story goes that *Magic: The Gathering* was designed to give players something to do in between D&D sessions, but it made much more money than anyone anticipated by inventing a whole new game genre—the collectible card game. Flush with cash, Wizards bought TSR and invited some of the remaining employees to move to Seattle from Wisconsin. There are still folks in the Seattle gaming industry today who made that move, and some of them went to work on a new edition of D&D.

Dungeons & Dragons third edition was published in 2000, and it changed the game. Again. While it was an innovative new system that ditched a lot of the mathematical oddness left over from the 1970s,[7] the main thing Wizards did differently for the community was to allow anyone, and I mean *anyone*, to use the basic framework of D&D in their own publications. Dubbed the d20 System and using an open gaming license (OGL) inspired by the open-source movement in software development, this led to an unprecedented boom in roleplaying game publishing and an expansion of the D&D community. There was a lot more D&D and D&D–adjacent roleplaying material available for fans of the game. Some was better, some was worse.[8]

The D&D community had grown up by this point. Many of those starry-eyed young people enamored by D&D in the late 1970s were now middle-aged. Gen Con had grown into a massive event, with more than fifty thousand attendees coming to play all kinds of board games, roleplaying games, and collectible card games. Outgrowing the convention center in Milwaukee, Wisconsin, Gen Con moved to Indianapolis in 2003, and never looked back. For

7. Greg: To this day, I still don't understand THAC0 and why high numbers of armor were less effective.

8. Greg: Please do not Google *Book of Erotic Fantasy*. Just don't.

some fans, traveling to a major convention like this was the only way to connect with other gamers and feel comfortable being themselves, rolling dice or bopping each other with foam swords. Sadly, though, the gatekeeping that marginalized groups experienced in the hobby continued, and while women and people of color attended Gen Con, the audience was still overwhelmingly white men.

The internet was where smaller communities began to thrive. Back then everyone's screen name was Durnan1491 or BadAssBeholder97. The anonymity of the early internet allowed people from more varied backgrounds access to D&D play and discussion that may have been closed to them because of their gender, sexual orientation, or the color of their skin. Forums and message boards had been around for a while, but the early 2000s saw an explosion of online communication that helped foster the next generation of D&D fans. The combination of a glut of RPG materials and easier access to community-gathering sites like the EN World forums or RPG.net allowed folks to be themselves more than ever. We started to see the D&D community slowly move toward acceptance of everyone, but we weren't there quite yet.

Another revision to the rules was published in 2003, and was called 3.5, which is totally not confusing at all! This is where Shelly and I enter the picture, although we didn't know each other yet. Shelly started working for Wizards in 1999, and while she was on the marketing team for Magic at first, she played her first D&D game six years later, in the Wizards office in Renton, Washington, using this edition. I graduated from college in 2000, and although I had played a few sessions of second edition AD&D in high school, it wasn't until I was living on my own in New York City in 2004 that I joined my first long-running campaign.

The Dungeon Master had an extremely wealthy spouse and invited us all to play D&D at his fancy apartment on the Upper West Side of Manhattan. He was excited to run us through the *Age of Worms* campaign published by Wizards in *Dragon* magazine from 2005 to 2006. The content in that magazine was developed by a company called Paizo (we'll get back to them later).

This campaign was eye-opening for many reasons. First, it allowed me to develop a character from level 1 all the way to level 22. Toddhedron was a half-elf ranger who was a lot like me, unsure of how to operate in this fandom that felt new to me. The DM was a longtime fan of the game and he loved introducing me to D&D lore from the 1980s I wasn't allowed to absorb back then because it was forbidden by my parents. I learned about Miska the Wolf-Spider and the Wind Dukes of Aaqa and how it all pertained to the

Rod of Seven Parts and the growing menace of Kyuss, an unholy deity. While I remember all that, I don't honestly recall a lot of the plot of the adventure path other than the characters my party-mates played and the professional relationships I made with them all.

That's right, nearly everyone I played with during that campaign I ended up working with in some creative capacity after it ended. One ended up working for Paizo. Another was a coauthor with me on three RPG books. Another I helped write a modern adaptation of a Molière script called *The Imaginary Invalid*, and together we produced it off-off-Broadway.

Most of all, I fell deeply in love with *Dungeons & Dragons* as a storytelling framework. We were as proud to have whole sessions centered around roleplaying our characters in a dramatic scene as the sessions describing the bombastic battles we barely won. I wrote fiction around one of the character's resurrections late in the campaign. Our group wasn't without interpersonal problems, and I learned how to deal with strong personalities by playing once a week or so for about three years. We developed a wonderful story together that will forever be my first ideal D&D play experience.

What made the group fall apart was the same thing that led to a fracturing of the D&D community in 2008: the publication of the fourth edition of *Dungeons & Dragons*. One of the players of our group was a freelancer working for Wizards on what would be the next edition of the game. We got access to the playtest material and played it pretty vigorously because we were excited to try something new. I volunteered to be the DM for the playtest since I hadn't done it before and I thought it would be good to jump in during the edition change.

There was just one problem. We hated it. D&D fourth edition changed the way the game was played a little too much for most of the group's tastes. Combat was bogged down, despite purporting to be a simpler system. You had to play it with miniatures on a grid of one-inch squares because so many of the rules involved pushing and pulling "squares" instead of the less abstract measurement of feet in earlier editions. Also (and this is a little hard to explain so bear with me), the abilities your wizard or fighter could do in combat were cool, but they were only explained in game terms, so the system encouraged a stricter interpretation. Our group was stumped by whether an ability that caused fire damage, for example, could actually ignite fires or if that was just flavor. Some DMs ruled that you couldn't use these abilities outside of combat against monsters, which I thought was ridiculous.

The D&D community was split on the new edition. There had always been purists who loved AD&D or who fondly held onto their second edition books even when a new edition was released. But once more fans played D&D fourth edition, the cracks in the community ruptured into full-on chasms. At the same time, people who worked at Wizards of the Coast weren't cool with letting anyone publish D&D material using the open gaming license of the third edition anymore, and they tried to let that idea die on the vine. Wizards eventually released the gaming system license (GSL) right before the new core rulebooks were released in 2008, and no one in the community was really happy about how it restricted use of the new edition.

This included the game designers at Paizo, who took their ball (expertise from working on *Dragon* magazine for the previous few years) and went home. They published a revised version of D&D 3.5 under the old license and called it *Pathfinder Roleplaying Game*. That game further created divisions in the RPG community by having a "new" game with innovations earned from a public playtest incorporating changes to D&D the community had long been wanting.

One thing the fourth edition accomplished that was actually popular was the delivery of new rules and a character builder you could access online. D&D Insider was a subscription service that gave the community access to everything Wizards published online, and it included a robust character and encounter builder that made prepping for each session much easier. Unfortunately, it was one step forward, two steps back, since you could only build your character using official material published by Wizards in the online tools. Third-party material like the books I was writing for Goodman Games, for example, didn't sell very well because you had to build your characters with pen and paper only. Since D&D was fairly complex and society had become exceedingly digital by then, nobody really wanted to do that.

This was a tough period for the D&D crowd, and they talked about it. A lot. Usually online in forums or on blogs. "Edition wars" was the term repeated ad nauseum within the community, and it was honestly pretty tiring in hindsight. You had fourth edition fans in one corner who loved everything Wizards was doing, criticisms be damned. You had Pathfinder stans in the other, supporting the underdog in the industry taking big swings. You had the Old School Renaissance folks (OSR if you're nasty) who went back to the basics of the first D&D game published in the 1970s and started tinkering with that rule set to return to that feel, complete with black-and-white rule books and line drawings for artwork. Some people jumped ship completely and started playing more video games or board games as a pastime instead of the wonders of roleplaying.

I was hired as a game journalist for a website called The Escapist in late 2009, primarily writing video game news and reviews. I think I only got the job because I had a few RPG credits on my résumé, and the publisher was an amateur D&D fanatic. Even though my concentration was supposed to be about games you played on the Xbox, PC, or PlayStation, I constantly pitched stories around D&D and the tabletop community. When the new D&D Red Box came out in 2010 to herald the start of a new line of Essentials books aimed at healing some of the chasms in the community, I wanted to start a lunchtime D&D campaign with my coworkers. I quickly had twelve volunteers, so I was running two campaigns set in the same fantasy world. Both groups started off strong with tons of laughing and rolling of dice in between bites of a ham and swiss from Subway. We stopped playing shortly after one group decided not to save the village and rampaging goblins burned it to the ground. I feel like there's a metaphor for something in there, but I don't know what exactly.

The years 2008 to 2012 were a toxic period in the D&D community. There were factions that didn't see eye to eye about, well, anything, but something emerged from this chaos and that was a growing notoriety among online personalities in the community. Some were analyzing the game and approaching it with a loving, critical eye. Some started creating and selling their own adventure modules, maps, campaign settings, fan art, cosplay, and even needlepoint. Others were pointing out D&D's many flaws. Loudly. Still others started recording their discussions on the game and putting it out in podcast form. Like someone named Bart Carroll who worked at Wizards of the Coast. Put a pin in that; we'll get back to it.

What's worth pointing out here is that the cultural medium of "being online" in the D&D community began during this period. You could become "internet famous" in various RPG communities. You could influence people before anybody used the term "influencers." It led to someone at Wizards speaking to someone at Penny Arcade, a webcomic-producing pair of Seattleites who also started a popular convention called PAX,[9] to join the D&D team

---

9. Greg: PAX (originally called the Penny Arcade Expo) is a series of gaming conventions held in several locations around the world. The first one was held in the Seattle area in 2004, and it grew into multiple annual events in the United States and Australia. PAX East is held in Boston, traditionally in the spring.

for a podcast, recording their first session together in 2008. That was called *Acquisitions Incorporated* after the party's name for themselves, and it was the first time many people listened to an unedited session of D&D for entertainment. It let fans hear how fun D&D was when you were hanging out with funny people.[10]

The content that began to be created around D&D in the online community allowed much more visibility for everyone, especially those who had been pushed out of the community before. For the first time, you didn't really have to travel on the convention circuit to develop a fan base, although that certainly helped. For the first time, it was very visible who was playing D&D, and that included a lot more women, queer people, and people of color than ever before. They were always there. They always enjoyed D&D, but now they could see each other. They started bringing their friends in because there's something special about this game. There really is.

More people than ever before were about to discover this, but something drastic needed to happen. Even though D&D still commanded the most brand recognition in tabletop RPGs, commonly held wisdom even among veteran journalists I spoke to was that Wizards of the Coast wasn't sure whether *Dungeons & Dragons* was going to be successful in the long run.

D&D needed to unite the disparate fan groups in the community. Luckily, Shelly and the rest of the D&D team had something cooked up by the time 2012 was about to roll around. Nathan Stewart was hired at Wizards of the Coast that year to lead the D&D business, and he fully supported the plan devised by Liz Schuh and the D&D designers as a really strong way to get everyone on board.

In December 2011, the D&D team at Wizards invited me to their headquarters in Renton, Washington, to learn, well, something. The PR team was very vague. I had gotten to know them over the past few years covering D&D for The Escapist. I made a point to meet up with them at events we were both attending even when they didn't have anything to show because when you are forced to report on games you personally find distasteful, you carve out time for the few you are truly interested in. D&D was one of those for me. I wasn't sure what to expect about this visit, however. All I knew is that a small

10. Shelly: Listening to these podcasts was how I learned how to play fourth edition D&D.

number of journalists and bloggers would be invited to the Wizards office to play with someone on the D&D team.

That's when I learned about D&D Next.[11] The team planned to run a massive public playtest for D&D by sending out a new version of the rules and collecting player feedback in a more holistic, scientific way through surveys and analytics. They were prepared to carve out parts of the game that people didn't like, leaving in what the most people loved, and return to a game that felt like it was made by the players. I got to play that first version of D&D before the playtest was announced, and it felt like a breath of fresh air. I met some folks in the community for the first time on that trip, including Ethan Gilsdorf who was gracious enough to quote me in the *New York Times* article he wrote on the experience at Wizards. I later tapped him to join a PAX East panel a few months later in 2012.

More than 180,000 fans participated in the playtest over the next couple of years. That fresh air I mentioned smelled really good to a great many within the D&D community. Not everyone loved every rule, but allowing fans to see the framework develop over the course of a few years helped create investment. The rules felt like the best parts of every previous edition of the game, plus some quirky new additions that were really innovative and fun, like rolling with advantage—that is, rolling two d20s and taking the better result.

Dungeons & Dragons published the fifth edition of the three core rule books, *Player's Handbook*, *Monster Manual*, and *Dungeon Master's Guide* in 2014 and led players on a story of the Cult of the Dragon attempting to resurrect Tiamat, their chromatic dragon goddess, with an adventure called *Hoard of the Dragon Queen*. A fancy cinematic trailer for the D&D storyline called Tyranny of Dragons was a pretty cool idea, and it set the tone for how story, lore, and above all entertainment through characters would be the focus for this edition. Given how well the playtest went, most fans thought D&D fifth edition would be incredibly fun to play, but no one predicted it would be so fun to watch. That was about to take off like a rocket ship.

Remember the podcast *Acquisitions Incorporated*? Well, the core group kept playing together for a few sessions of audio-recorded amazingness, and they added Wil Wheaton, an actor you may remember from *Star Trek: The Next*

11. Shelly: I am 99.9 percent sure that I came up with the name D&D Next. I used it as a placeholder in a meeting, and it caught on.

Generation or the film *Stand by Me*. They put aside their microphones and head-sets in 2010 and played D&D in front of an audience at the Paramount Theater in Seattle during PAX. People had played D&D with an audience watching at gaming conventions and events in the past, but it was usually a bunch of former game designers or fantasy authors. It could certainly get raucous, and people enjoyed it for sure. Two things changed in 2010 that forever altered the way live D&D play performances were perceived. First, the notoriety of the players began to reach other fandoms of internet famous folks from the Star Trek, web comics, and video game universes and bring some of those fans back to pay attention to D&D. Second, the concept of an ongoing story with D&D characters that persisted through the podcast and to live performances was novel. Third was Chris Perkins coming into his own as a performer and storyteller. Okay, fine! Three things!

Seriously, Perkins's charisma was a big reason these events were so popular. He was already one of the longest-tenured game designers working on D&D and he embraced his role as "DM to the Stars" despite not quite believing people came to watch him and the *Acquisitions Incorporated* crew joke around for a couple hours. Perkins, community manager Trevor Kidd, and the production crew at Penny Arcade ramped up their skills over the years so that these gaming sessions started to feel like full-on theater productions with animated intros, custom-made miniature scenery, lighting cues, smoke machines, and costumes. Perkins played hilarious characters and terrifying villains to bounce off the curmudgeonly camaraderie at the table. By the time 2014 and the fifth edition of *Dungeons & Dragons* was out there, and everyone was talking about dragons, queens, and the hoards that bind them, Chris Perkins took the stage at the Benaroya Hall dressed in purple robes and a dragon headdress. He expertly wove a tale for the group that night, which included an aerial dragon fight from the deck of an airship. The audience ate it up.

The people in the seats had been watching these performers for years and followed them like an indie band or something. A strange call and response thing developed where if Perkins described something as a fire with a green flame, for example, the audience would yell, "Green flame!" The first time you experience that while sitting in the audience is freaking surreal, let me tell you. It feels like you missed the memo and you can't really fathom how uniformly the audience repeats that phrase. There was almost no laughter afterward, so this chorus of 3,000 fans said the words "green flame" in almost perfect unison, and Perkins immediately went back to describing the action on the battlefield. It was disconcerting. And magical.

The D&D team put the video for these games up on YouTube, and they've earned millions of views. Watching it live, and then seeing those numbers go up was when I was certain the D&D community was poised to grow. I was hired at Wizards of the Coast by Nathan Stewart about nine months after the fifth edition was released, in March 2015. That same week, *Critical Role* debuted on the Geek & Sundry network on Twitch,[12] the video streaming platform that was recently acquired by Amazon for almost a billion dollars. Coincidence? I think so! But I quickly saw that content created around D&D would be a huge way to connect with the community, just like "green flame!" connected with the *Acquisitions Incorporated* audience. There was a way for our marketing team at D&D to get out there and continue to unite the clans.

Shelly was on a panel I moderated at PAX East in 2012, and we stayed in contact. I ran into her once or twice after that, but we *really* hit it off when my wife and I came to visit the Wizards offices before we moved to Seattle. I remember walking into the lobby with the huge display of Mitzi the dragon and locked eyes with . . . R. A. Salvatore. "What are you doing here?" Bob asked a little threateningly in his thick Boston accent. "Uh, I work here now," I said. After he gave me shit for always being a tough interview when I talked to him about video game stuff over the years, we introduced our wives to each other and marveled at the weirdness of life that put us in this moment. Then we complained about the Red Sox a little.

I started work a week or so later, but there honestly wasn't very much for me to do right away. I was hungry to prove myself, so when Shelly mentioned that they were recording a podcast, I raised my head with a look on my face that was half-crestfallen and half-expectant. Does she like me? Does she want to work with me on something? Anything? I don't think she was going to do this until she saw that look, but Shelly asked if I wanted to join them. I actually jumped out of my seat and ended up being the (checks notes) fourth host on an interview with the designers of a D&D board game that was coming out.

There eventually was a lot more for me to do for the brand. In addition to moving the D&D podcast to releasing weekly and working with the team on rebranding it to *Dragon Talk*, I started to realize there was a huge potential

12. Greg: *Critical Role* was a home game of six prolific voice actors from anime and video games who improvised an extremely well-imagined type of D&D. Felicia Day, actor and founder of Geek & Sundry, thought it would be entertaining for people to watch these performers play their game for an audience, similar to what Wil Wheaton had done on *Acquisitions Incorporated*. *Critical Role* is very popular to this day.

in working with fans already in the entertainment industry to bring more visibility to D&D. We worked on launching more streaming live play shows produced internally, including one around a vampire gothic horror adventure called *Curse of Strahd* in early 2016. The players in the group didn't know each other before we put them together with Chris Perkins, but they brought their own fans from YouTube, Twitch, and other social media followings. The audience for watching people play D&D continued to grow.

So I got to thinking, what if we put geeky actors together with the streaming talent in L.A. that was approaching more professionalism due to the ease of broadcasting online and brought them under the hood on some great D&D storylines the team was making? Would that catapult the success D&D was seeing in the book sales even further?

It can't be overstated how awesome the fifth edition core rulebooks truly are at bringing more people into the game. As the lead rules developer, Jeremy Crawford was instrumental in increasing LGBTQIA+ representation explicitly in the rules. He also worked closely with Kate Irwin and the other art directors to make sure queer people, women, and people of color were depicted in the illustrations of the fifth edition just as much as white male characters were. Chainmail bikinis were banned, melted in protest, and replaced with more depictions of these individuals as heroes. The archetype for a human fighter in the *Player's Handbook* is a Black woman with locs. The whole look and feel of the edition with its redesigned ampersand logo and red graphic stylings on the masterfully illustrated covers (art directed by Shauna Wolf Narciso) made the books feel modern and cool.

Everyone wanted D&D books on their shelves, including the burgeoning (and formerly underground) nerd comedy scene in Los Angeles. I worked with an awesome team on an event called D&D Live from Meltdown in 2016, which brought folks to the Meltdown Comics (R.I.P.) store on Sunset Boulevard in Hollywood. Designers from the D&D team were there talking up their work alongside video game designers from *Neverwinter*[13] and comedians like Brian Posehn and Jonah Ray, who often performed at the small stage in the back of the comic shop. We introduced the group Force Grey at this event, DMed by Matthew Mercer from *Critical Role*, and worked on a deal to distribute an edited video series of the group playing D&D together on the Nerdist channel.

---

13. Greg: *Neverwinter* is a MMO (massively multiplayer online game), but instead of orcs versus humans, it's set on the Sword Coast in the Forgotten Realms using mechanics inspired by D&D. There are some orcs too.

At the same time D&D was doing all this, the community of content creators making videos around the game continued to get bigger and bigger, like someone had cast *enlarge personality* on it. The high charisma of people creating content around the game was increasing around the world with groups from the United Kingdom, Australia, Mexico, or wherever playing together and posting their play experiences online. The *Critical Role* audience went from big to fricking huge in the blink of an eye. *Acquisitions Incorporated* started a weekly adventure with the *C-Team*. Women were playing more than ever in groups like Misscliks and Girls Guts Glory, which felt very empowering and engaging for all types of nonmasculine folks and encouraged those watching to start their own D&D groups.

At the same time, a community of new map makers, adventure designers, and D&D enthusiasts was embracing the fifth edition. The open gaming license idea of the third edition wasn't truly in effect anymore, but the spirit of fan-created D&D material that had roots all the way back to the 1970s was still going strong. Established RPG companies like Green Ronin and Kobold Press continued to publish D&D fifth edition stuff after being hired to develop some of the adventure material by Chris Perkins and the team in 2014 and 2015, just like the companies that spawned around TSR back in the day. Nathan Stewart believed there was an avenue for nurturing this kind of creativity while keeping it rooted in the D&D playground of the Forgotten Realms. He gave the green light to D&D team member Chris Lindsay and OneBookshelf to create a community marketplace called Dungeon Masters Guild. There anyone could use intellectual property that was previously held close to the vest by Wizards and put their creations up for sale to earn money through the increased visibility the DMs Guild could provide. Community standouts like Matt Mercer were among the first to publish their material on the site, and it quickly became the go-to place for up-and-coming D&D designers and creatives to show off their chops.

Taking all that momentum and goodwill in the present community, the D&D team doubled down with an even bigger event called the Stream of Annihilation in 2017. I invited a cross-section of the burgeoning D&D streaming community to a studio in Seattle and asked them to play different incarnations of the annual adventure we were plugging that year, called Tomb of Annihilation. For many, this gathering was the first time they had ever met face to face. As Matt Mercer said in the green room next door to the main studio, "This is the largest gathering of people with impostor syndrome that I've ever seen." More of them were hungry for any kind of validation for what they were doing, and simply being recognized (even applauded) by the company that makes one of their favorite games was incredibly meaningful.

And it worked! D&D books sold better in 2017 than they had in decades. Not only were people into the incredible storylines and excellently designed supplements the D&D team produced like *Xanathar's Guide to Everything*, but the core rulebooks were consistently selling well years after their release. Typically, when a new edition of the game comes out, there is a flurry of sales early on and then revenues taper off slowly. That just wasn't true for D&D fifth edition, and sales continued to go up and up and up. That meant that in addition to the D&D team creating awesome books, the work the marketing team was doing to engage the D&D community was successful in growing the audience into demographics that might have previously felt alienated. The books of D&D's fifth edition did a fantastic job of showing how varied and amazing the peoples you could embody looked and felt, and it was time for that message to be carried out in every event or live-stream the team planned.

The final bit that was missing, I think, was a more direct appeal to people of color to play more D&D. I mentioned at the start of this history that D&D as a brand didn't do very much to interest nonwhite people in playing the game. Those people often felt excluded from the community. As I was preparing to attempt to outdo the success of the Stream of Annihilation and speaking to more Black folks on *Dragon Talk*, I realized something pretty important. To end exclusion, I had to include. It was up to me to actively seek out talent from those communities and invite them to D&D events. So I did.

The Stream of Many Eyes in 2018 is my *Mona Lisa*, my *Dark Side of the Moon*, my *Hamilton*. I did not throw away my shot. We added a studio audience to the live D&D games we presented and sold a couple hundred tickets to fans to come and participate in the festivities. A set designer built a fantasy city block in a big studio in Hollywood with storefronts doubling as booth space for our partners. I worked with local stunt performers, renaissance fair professionals, makeup artists, and amazing cosplayers. All that awesomeness simulated what it might have felt like to be in Waterdeep, City of Splendor, where that year's D&D adventure book was set.

On the day before we let in people to see it for the first time, I walked onto the set and looked around at hundreds of people dressed as their D&D character and the make-believe world my efforts had somehow made tangible. For just a moment, the fantasy felt real.

And I wept. That's right, full on sobbed in the middle of a marketing event I was running. I moved to a little corner of the studio and just let the tears stream down my face. I couldn't believe we had pulled it off.

Oddly enough, that wasn't the only time I cried in public that weekend. I was moved by bringing a group of people of color to an official D&D event for the first time. I reached out to a guest of *Dragon Talk*, Tanya DePass, and in a few months we pulled together people of color in the Chicago area who were interested in learning more about D&D. *Rivals of Waterdeep* debuted at Stream of Many Eyes, and you can read more about the formation of that (and why I cried) in my essay with Tanya later in this book.

Since that time, I've made it a point to lift up voices from all over the community. Trans and gay people play D&D, drag queens play D&D, fashionable women who like *The Real Housewives* and *The Bachelor* play D&D the same as men who only watch action movies and go to the gym play D&D. All people love stories. All people play D&D. It was time to show that not just in the amazing art direction in the D&D books but in the promotion of the game everywhere.

I'm proud that *Dungeons & Dragons* continues to inspire people to come together, even when they can't do so physically. When the global pandemic hit in 2020, millions of people jumped online to play D&D and experience any kind of connection with their friends or family. Some of them had played D&D before, but a significant amount of folks started rolling dice for the first time when COVID forced them to stay home. Digital tools like *D&D Beyond* have made the game more accessible than ever, and new fans continue to flock to the game with 2020 continuing the trend of record-breaking popularity of D&D. Every human on the planet needs the type of connection that D&D can provide.

That's why Shelly and I get up in the morning and do what we do on *Dragon Talk* each week. We want to lift you up to be your best self, just like all the guests we talk to do in their own communities.

What's Your Origin Story? (Shelly)

There was a time in my life when I honestly believed I would be the ingenue on a popular soap opera, a dolphin trainer, and married to Sebastian Bach from the glorious 1980s hair band Skid Row. All these things were more conceivable than becoming the cohost of the official *Dungeons & Dragons* podcast.

I was not exposed to D&D growing up. Or at least I don't think I was. What little I knew about it was all stereotypes, which I allegedly weaponized to tease some of the boys in my class. I was exactly the kind of kid who would have loved D&D (minus the alleged teasing). I was a storyteller (or liar, as my mom would say), an inventor of friends (Monster with the Glasses, Red Monster, Chuckie Puckie Bunny Bear), and haver of too much free time. But alas, I didn't roll my first polyhedral die until it was required by my employer—who happened to be the game's publisher.

Many moons ago, I was hired as a promotions coordinator for *Magic: The Gathering*. Back in my day, games involved hungry hippos and buying and selling (and subsequently crying about) real estate. Cards did not attack one another. What was happening here? A few weeks into my employment, my boss sent me to College Station, Texas, for the D&D Silver Anniversary Tour.

"But I work on *Magic*!" I said. "Is that even allowed?"

Turns out, yes. Yes, it was. The events team was short-staffed, and you shouldn't say no to your boss less than a month into a new job.

The D&D Silver Anniversary Tour was a series of events around the country where fans got together at bookstores, played D&D, and hobnobbed with game designers and authors. What I discovered began to dissolve many of the antiquated stereotypes I had harbored since elementary school:

- With the exception of a dude cosplaying as ALF, no one wore a costume (then again, that may have been the guy's real hair).
- No one threw a chair or pulled out a calculator or seemed generally flummoxed by all that dang math.
- There were no candles, no swords, no sacrifices—at least not in real life. Oddly, I was somewhat disappointed by this.
- People were having fun. They were laughing. They seemed to like each other. But how was that possible with such a serious game?

I went to three of the Silver Anniversary's tour stops but didn't interact with D&D in a meaningful way again for many years.

My job changed often. I worked on almost every product Wizards of the Coast published in the 2000s. I eventually found my way to the D&D publishing team (and the incredible Liz Schuh, who hired me and remains one of my favorite Wizards) to work on the marketing for our newly launched children's book imprint, Mirrorstone. I loved working on the kids' books. Now *this* was a D&D I understood! I was slowly discovering what would become one of my biggest professional passions: introducing kids to *Dungeons & Dragons*. At some point I was asked if I played D&D.

"Ooooh, ha, no, but I read the books!" I said, grabbing my copy of *Dagger of Doom* and taking off.

A few new people joined the team, and unlike me, they weren't trying to hide their lack of D&D experience or pretend it wasn't needed to perform their job to the best of their abilities. Those goody-goodies were all like, "Ahhhhh, teach us the ways of dragon slaying! Ooooooh, please let us be Dungeon Masters so we can boss people around and steal their loot!" (Or whatever it was Dungeon Masters did.) So an introductory game was formed and a meeting was scheduled. I was on the invite along with a note from Teddy, the DM. "Liz said you have to learn how to play D&D."

Oh fine.

I met with Teddy before the game to roll up my first character. This was back in 3.5 edition, so after approximately 1,838 hours, a lot of pencil shavings, many dice rolled, and so much math, I had a character: an elf sorceress.

Teddy handed me a miniature from his collection. "Here, use this."

The fantasy me had long, blonde hair and lovely pink robes. She brandished a staff in her right hand.

"I shall call her Astrid," I said, petting her plastic hair. I was in love.

As I took a seat at the table with my coworkers, I flashed back to that afternoon in Texas where I witnessed my first game of D&D. Why did this moment feel like those split seconds between getting strapped into your seat on Space Mountain and the ride blasting off? The excitement was palpable. We were no longer brand managers and ad traffickers and project managers. We were rogues and rangers and clerics. We weren't seven people who barely knew each other and used interoffice mail as our main mode of communication. We were an adventuring party. By the end of that first game, we were best friends.

I was so overwhelmed by the incredible experience I just had playing *Dungeons & Dragons* and full of contrition for all the misguided things I once thought about my new favorite game that I wrote an essay about my secret life as an elf and gave it to an editor I had worked with at the *Seattle Times*. She had published articles of mine about speed dating hijinks and one time that I baked sugar cookies that almost killed people, but this one was a hard pass.

"What is this?" she asked. "I have no idea what you're doing. Is this a game? Are you okay?"

But I was determined. If I was so wrong about D&D, there had to be other women out there like me. D&D *was* a game for us! Those nerdy brainiacs with the goofy haircuts in third grade were right! (Okay, fine, I did make fun of them!) This game was fun. It was exactly what my friends and I do when we're together: tell stories, support each other, celebrate our victories, banish eeeeevil, eat snacks! I gave my essay to Liz, who passed it on to the head of R&D, who decided I was on to something. Turned out there was already talk about making D&D feel more accessible to a larger audience. I wrote a book proposal—part how-to, part personal essay—geared toward women like myself who never fancied themselves as roleplayers. The proposal became my first book about D&D called *Confessions of a Part-Time Sorceress: A Girl's Guide to Dungeons & Dragons*. I wrote another D&D book that was published in 2011 called *Everything I Need to Know I Learned from Dungeons & Dragons: One Woman's Quest to Trade Elf-Help for Self-Help*. So yeah, I guess I like writing and talking about *Dungeons & Dragons*. Who would have thought?

Oh, right. You wanted to hear about *Dragon Talk*'s origin story.

Like all good D&D adventures, *Dragon Talk*'s beginning is shrouded in mystery. One day some designers from the R&D department had the idea to start a podcast, according to Bart Carroll, senior digital marketing manager at Wizards and the only person left who knows how this thing started. This was back in the third edition era, and we didn't have a "podcast department" or even a social media team. Bart was working on the D&D website and was tasked with exploring all sorts of new platforms, so it fell to him. (He liked a challenge, as evidenced by the fact that he married me.)

The very first episode of "the D&D Podcast" (as it was known then; it was years before Greg officially christened it *Dragon Talk*) was recorded in a storage room because it was the only room at the office with a locking door. They didn't do interviews, it was just D&D designers talking about rules and mechanics, which, yeah, I know, sounds really cool. Bart knew nothing about audio engineering, so obviously he was the perfect person to lead this charge. Armed with a simple microphone setup, a laptop, GarageBand, and a randomly sourced audio board (only about 6 percent of its levers and switches were actually used), Bart somehow managed to record a podcast, edit it, and get it up on the digital airwaves.

Trying to up his audio game, Bart ordered egg crate foam for soundproofing, which was pinned straight into the drywall. That worked okay until the custodial service took it all down, believing it was garbage. This remained the podcast studio for years.

Those early podcasts were sporadically scheduled. It was hard to get people to commit because of work, even though their day jobs were about sixteen feet from the makeshift studio. More than once, they lost half of the episodes already posted because of "quirks in the system." While the podcast was fun, it wasn't anyone's priority, so it tended to get left on the back burner.

Then the studio had to move because that only locked room in the building was turning into an office for a new exec. The podcast had to go on the road for a while, recording in conference rooms or the empty offices of vacationing coworkers. The podcast responsibility shifted from R&D to marketing, which is how I got involved, but no one remembers how or why I ended up hosting. Now, I know my memory is garbage. I only remember theme songs from 1980s sitcoms and the phone number of my favorite pizza place from when I was a kid, so I'm not surprised that I don't recall the first time I recorded an episode. I think it was in 2013, but I suspect I made at least a couple of appearances in 2012. But literally no one remembers. Was I there all along? Did I forget a few years? Was I really a part-time sorceress?

There were other hosts. Trevor Kidd was one for a while. Bart ended up doing it too. Sometimes all three of us hosted and sometimes just one. We had zero acoustics in our roving studio, which meant that sometimes the sound of a toilet flushing or a hallway door slamming could be heard in the background because no one knew how to edit that out. Occasionally a co-worker would wander in while we were recording, put their laptop and bottle of water on the table, and take a seat, not realizing they were in the wrong room or that we were in the middle of recording a podcast.

We interviewed local designers and visiting freelancers. If someone sent me an email asking to support an event that sounded fun, we would interview them too. I always tried to do research and come up with a list of questions ahead of time. I'd give them to Trevor and Bart and they'd be like, "Cool. Thanks, nerd," and go off the cuff.

Somehow Bart wrangled a small budget for the podcast, which allowed him to hire an actual producer/engineer. We had a handful of contractors come and go, but a guy named Joshua stood out. We could tell he was a pro because he was appalled by our ragtag recording setup. He did his best to help us by offering interview tips, equipment upgrade suggestions, and even bringing in an old, crocheted blanket that he gently laid on the conference room table, attempting to better the acoustics. He left us after only a few weeks to take a producer job at KUOW, Seattle's NPR station. I still hear him all the time on the radio.

The good news about Joshua's departure was that it opened the door for

Ryan Marth. During his interview, Bart asked Ryan if he liked D&D. Ryan said, "Never played, but I do like clean audio." Bart hired him on the spot.

Ryan's first recording was on January 14, 2015. It was an episode about DM appreciation—a month-long holiday celebrating Dungeon Masters I initiated but failed to make an annual event. (I really did try though, DMs.) Things were definitely improving with Ryan on board, and they were about to get a whole lot better.

I knew Greg because of his role as editor in chief at The Escapist. We didn't meet until PAX East in 2012, when we joined Ethan Gilsdorf and John Stavropoulos on a panel called "How to Start Playing D&D." Greg was so nice and friendly, and I was so nervous and awkward. So really, nothing's changed.

A few years later, Greg got hired as communications manager for D&D and was making the move from North Carolina to Washington. One day, before his start date, I ran into him and his wife, Erin, in the lobby. I was with Bob Salvatore[14] and they were with then senior director (now vice president) for D&D, Nathan Stewart. I knew at that moment Greg and I would become great friends and spend lots of time together because Erin and I hit it off big time and there would be no keeping us apart.

Greg's desk was right next to mine. One afternoon I interrupted him to say that if he wasn't busy, he should join us on the podcast. It seemed like a fitting invitation for our new communications manager. He sat in as a third or fourth host (our hosts to guest ratio was totally out of whack back then) on a few interviews and we even put him in the hot seat as an interviewee. Then Bart got moved to the Magic team and was no longer able to work on D&D projects, and Trevor kind of phased himself out, so all that remained in those double-booked, acoustic-challenged conference rooms were Greg, Ryan, and myself.

"Guess you're the hosts now," Ryan said.

Greg must have been thinking, *Oh hell no! If I'm going to do this, we need to step it up! Did someone just flush the toilet? Nooooooooo!*

But really, he wanted to.

His first suggestion was to name the podcast something with a bit more pizzazz. Yeah, it was technically a D&D podcast, but it wasn't the only one out there. It was, however, the only one that could be called "the official

---

14. Shelly: *New York Times* best-selling author of The Legend of Drizzt series and many more. No bigs. Just hanging out with best-selling authors at the office.

Dungeons & Dragons podcast," so we started using that tagline, along with the new name, *Dragon Talk*, in every episode.

His next suggestion was to put out episodes on a regular basis. At the time, our release cadence was what I believe is known in the industry as "willy nilly." Greg correctly noted that if we wanted people to find the podcast and build an audience, we had to release the same day of the week, every week.

The D&D community was made up of a varied and diverse cast of characters with different specializations and backgrounds. We decided to make guest interviews the focus of the show so we could highlight these efforts. A troop leader who created an RPG badge for his local Girl Scouts chapter, a therapist using D&D in their practice, a high school English teacher who used D&D in the classroom—we loved them all. We couldn't shake a staff of bird calls without encountering hugely talented people lending their skills to the D&D community. Streamers, designers, cartographers, Dungeon Masters, cosplayers, artists, all working toward creating wholly immersive and entertaining experiences centered around *Dungeons & Dragons*.

In 2016, Greg introduced our first recurring shorter form segment, "Lore You Should Know." Inspired by the *Stuff You Should Know* podcast, "Lore You Should Know" (or LYSK as it's known) was meant to appeal to general D&D fans who wanted a deep dive on the story behind the stories. Greg sat down with D&D designers such as Chris Perkins, Adam Lee, and Ari Levitch and peppered them with questions about topics ranging from etiquette in the Feywild to Warlock Genie Patrons to the enemies of Illithids. It was a bit self-serving, as Greg was genuinely curious about the Forgotten Realms— the fifth edition's default setting—but he figured he wasn't the only one. It was hugely well received and remains our most popular segment.

Then Hollywood came knocking—or rather, we knocked and Hollywood answered. Turns out Tinseltown was teeming with former and current dragon delvers. People were saying "yes" to the official *Dungeons & Dragons* podcast. Actors, directors, musicians, screenwriters, animators, showrunners, and authors. These people were showing up in my *E!News* feed one week and on my laptop over Skype the next. Not only were they playing D&D, but they were also crediting the game with how they got the chops to be successful in their field. Dungeon Mastering taught worldbuilding and plot pacing. Heroes learned character development and honed performance skills. We were all part of this same, strange, starting-to-bubble-up subculture connected by a game of make-believe.

The podcast kept going because no one told us to stop. In fact, we got a few more resources and a tiny budget to buy a few pieces of furniture and set items from the IKEA down the street. We got Sean Mayovsky to help produce part-time and a dedicated studio space! No more double-booked conference rooms. Live-streaming was starting to become a priority, so the company let us take over an empty office and even put a lock on the door. We shared the room with the Magic team, who were doing more in-house production work (including their own podcast). *Dragon Talk* was still audio only, which suited me just fine, but I kept hearing rumblings about maybe turning on a camera while we were recording to see what happened. I hated the idea. I was already a nervous Nellie before the interviews and the guests couldn't even see me. Now I'd have to worry about strangers on the internet watching us and being able to comment on my terrible posture and double chin. I kept fighting it, and Greg kept appeasing me, but I had a feeling it was a losing battle.

The popularity of LYSK spurred the creation of more short-form segments. "Sage Advice" was born from the popular column of the same name where lead rules designer Jeremy Crawford and Greg discussed not just how to play but the intent behind the rules. DMs are free, even encouraged, to make up their own rules if it makes the game more fun at the table.

I had a terrifying DM experience. I laboriously overplanned every detail of my one-shot adventure and immediately crumbled and never regained composure because my players zoomed to the left when I expected them to go right. That was almost ten years ago and I've been too gun-shy to take the mantle behind the screen again. (But I really want to, and I think I'm close.) "How to DM" (HtDM) is my self-serving segment where I talk to experienced Dungeon Masters and steal all their powers. Know what you do if your players go left when you thought they'd go right? Move everything to the left! Learned that from "How to DM."

"Random Character Generator" showed off one of the greatest parts of D&D—creating a character! Greg and other members of the D&D team sit down together to generate random characters (as the name suggests) on *D&D Beyond* and improvise a backstory for the character over the course of the segment. They make great NPCs!

"Insight Check" is a newer segment, and it was designed to not just give listeners an introduction to the many talented people who work in the D&D studio and other departments within Wizards, but mostly as a way for Greg and me to get to know and catch up with coworkers while we were working from home during COVID. We hired a bunch of new people and only knew them as faces on a computer screen. There are lots of passionate, talented people with cool jobs on our team, and fans love the behind-the-scenes look at how the rothé sausage gets made.[15]

I finally lost the live-stream battle, but we gained Pelham Greene, who came on board to help with streaming, camera operation, and moderating the chat (i.e., making sure I never saw those comments about my double chin). Every Friday before we recorded, Sean had to rearrange the room because it was used by many teams on a multitude of projects. He had to roll the tiny round table we begged out of facilities to the center of the room and cover it with the ill-fitted black rectangular tablecloth we borrowed from the events department. He swapped out the Magic art so we could have a D&D background. He worked with Pelham to set up the mics and place the huge jar of d20s on the table so Greg could knock them over at the end of the episode when he declares, "Rocks fall, everyone dies!"

We had people listening and watching. We got to know our friends in chat who joined us every afternoon. We always felt like we were doing a service by bringing amazing work by talented people to a larger audience. Occasionally Nathan Stewart, head of D&D, would crash the studio during recording and just shake his head and walk out. Later, he would ask if we ever discussed D&D on the "official D&D podcast" because all he ever heard was terrible character impressions and poop talk. Deep down we know he liked it too. Very deep down, but it was there.

At the end of 2018, *Dragon Talk* got another win when Ryan hired his former intern and friend, Lisa Carr, for production assistance. While Greg was busy changing what listeners were hearing, Lisa changed the behind-the-scenes presentation. She researched prospective guests and handled the bookings. She prepared detailed lead sheets on every guest based on her pre-interviews. She made sure guests had technical help and knew how to call in or, if they were coming to the office, always had a friendly face to meet them in the lobby. You guys, this was some *Good Morning America*–level professionalism. Lisa's involvement continues to be legendary. We literally could not do the show without her.

---

15. Shelly: Rothés are herd animals commonly found in the Underdark. I picked them because they're the most cow-like, but I'm also a vegetarian, so I could be way off here.

In 2020 when the pandemic hit, we were sent home from the office and told to come back in two weeks. Not wanting to miss recording, Pelham got a bunch of equipment sent to our homes, and Ryan walked us through how to set everything up over Zoom. Our basements and guest rooms turned into mini studios. Two weeks turned into eighteen months (and counting). Our tiny home internet connections couldn't handle the live-streaming, so we paused that and started recording the episodes for YouTube instead. As the D&D fandom continued to grow, so did the content creators. There was a new D&D podcast or live-stream popping up daily. There was no shortage of guests.

Thanks to Lisa and Ryan and everyone who worked on *Dragon Talk*, in 2021 we celebrated our 300th episode! We did a special live show and a bunch of our past guests recorded special congratulatory messages that made Greg and me cry. For 300 episodes we remained true to our mission to "lift up" the diverse and sometimes underrecognized voices and shine a spotlight on their work and the positive effect they make every day.[16] We'll do it for 300 more episodes if no one tells us to stop. We wanted listeners to learn about a new stream or D&D supplement or how to hire someone to run a D&D–themed birthday party for your kid. The essays gathered here represent just that. These were the ones that popped into our minds as soon as we got the official greenlight to write this book because they represent the cross-section of the D&D community. These are the ones that continued to inspire us long after the interview was over. These are the ones listeners wrote to us about to tell us how much they related or how excited they were to discover someone's work. Most important, these are the ones that show the world that no matter who you are or where you came from, you will always have a seat at our table.

16. Shelly: "Lift you up" is our unofficial mission statement and something Greg and I say a lot on *Dragon Talk* because of how the D&D community supports and promotes each other's work.

Matthew Lillard Goes Off the Rails

The first time Matthew Lillard was on *Dragon Talk*, I interviewed him on my own, and from the get-go it was one of the most off-the-rails interviews on the show. Shelly was sipping sparkling wine on vacation in West Palm Beach or something and missed all the fun! Matt was a joy to speak with and not just because his jokes about day drinking during the opening moments made me feel pretty comfortable. Many of you dear readers may recognize Matt from his roles in TV and film—there are way too many credits to list here. Seriously, there are like, way too many. It was fun talking to such an accomplished actor and showcasing how he belongs in the D&D community along with all the rest of us nerds.

But my story with Matt doesn't begin with that interview. I actually met him around six months earlier, in March 2017 at a coffee shop in the shadow of Warner Bros. Studios like I was some real Hollywood professional PR person. I was busy recruiting folks all over L.A. for a D&D event that ended up being called the Stream of Annihilation. I had heard from Liz Schuh that he was into D&D, and even though it was a long shot, I reached out to the email address she gave me to see if he would be willing to chat. Matt was kind enough to take a meeting and suggested we have breakfast in Studio City.

It was a bright, sunny day. The white buildings reflected so much light that I was thankful I'd splurged on Ray-Bans for this trip. I got to the restaurant a little early and put my name in for a table. I walked back out and scanned the outside dining area to make sure Matt hadn't sat down before me. I noticed a short, bearded man looking at me as he sat across from a woman and a small baby. Turning back around, I was surprised to hear someone say, "Greg?"

I looked back at the guy with the baby and recognized him as someone I hadn't seen in years. I went to college with Bobby Moynihan in Connecticut and was super excited when he landed *Saturday Night Live* in 2008. He even invited some of us to a show at 30 Rock, and I got to go to a real SNL after-party with the whole cast and host Seth Rogen. But that's a different story. . . .

Bobby was sitting at the table with his wife and their brand-new daughter. He beamed at seeing me and we hugged, saying how strange it was to meet up here of all places. We chatted a little bit, and I was able to hold his daughter for a few moments before I saw that Matt had arrived. I didn't want to make it weird and say I had to go talk to another famous actor, so I just politely said I was meeting somebody and it was so great to see them and we have to get together again soon.

With an already surreal moment like that under my belt at 9 a.m. on a weekday, I was suddenly sitting across a table from Matthew Lillard. Like many of you, I grew up watching *Hackers*, *Scream*, *SLC Punk*, and countless other films he's been in over the years. What I didn't know was that during that whole time he had been playing D&D with the same group of actors he met in theater school back in 1990. They still played together on the regular, and although he was the only one still acting in the business, they were thinking of creating a business together centered around their shared love of D&D.

I thought I was pitching to Matt during this meeting, but I later realized he was actually pitching to me!

We talked about the D&D business a bunch and how I would love for him to be a part of the Stream of Annihilation before moving on to our shared history with theater and acting. He wanted to know about my background— my descriptions of trying to make it in NYC with standup comedy and downtown theater productions resonated with him. At one point, Matt looked at me and said, "Oh, so you're a creative. Got it." I had never been prouder of my past work!

After that meeting, Matt agreed to come to Seattle to play D&D for the event, but only if we could bring his buddies too. Travel for five was an easy ask to fulfill, and that's how they all ended up rolling dice with Matthew Mercer and Joe Manganiello during the Stream of Annihilation. During that event, Matt pitched the concept of high-end collector's editions to Nathan Stewart, our boss on D&D, on a street corner in Seattle's Belltown neighborhood. It was a little out of left field for a bunch of friends to start a business together, but something about that outside-the-box pitch from Matt landed somewhere solid. A deal was struck. Four years later, he and his four friends now run a company called Beadle & Grimm's that makes platinum editions of D&D adventures with physical accessories to enhance gameplay, and it all started with me meeting him at that coffee shop.

The first time Matt came on *Dragon Talk* was in fall 2017, a few months after Stream of Annihilation. I brought him into the studio Wizards had recently built out of a small office, and I honestly didn't know what to expect for this recording. Shelly wasn't there, so I didn't have my wingwoman, er, cohost. I wasn't nervous, really, because Matt and I had built up a rapport already. I had nothing to worry about. Like when we first met, it was a gracious surprise that he asked me questions about my history as much he wanted to talk about himself. I appreciated the good-natured ribbing of how handsome production associate Pelham Greene was or how I named my first long-term D&D character Todd. (It was actually Toddhedron and he was called Toad 99 percent of the time but the point stands, dude.)

A few moments stand out from this interview. Matt's story of being fortunate enough to be at the premiere of *Return of the King* in New Zealand sitting next to fellow actor Abraham Benrubi and seeing the tears streaming down his face at the conclusion meant that Abraham was worthy enough to join Matt's D&D game. The anecdote of his teenage kids playing D&D with friends and how the game ends up being instructive in how to act as a human was inspirational to me and my own young children. It was cool to hear how he plays D&D in L.A. with a bunch of TV showrunners and how that game runs totally differently than the one he plays with his group of longtime friends. Matt also had just done the first table read for *Good Girls* right before this interview and had just done *Twin Peaks* season 3, so it's a cool snapshot of where his acting career was in 2017.

Shelly and I have spoken to Matt a bunch of times since that first interview. Leading up to the next big D&D event, the Stream of Many Eyes in 2018, we spoke to him and Mark Hulmes, since Matt was going to play in his session.[1] Matt's enthusiasm for re-creating the fantasy city blocks of Waterdeep was palpable. His excitement was honestly a great boon to me as someone who is not always confident about their creative work, and this event was a big

---

1. Greg: Mark Hulmes is an amazing British DM for a streaming show called *High-Rollers*, among others, and an awesome person in their own right.

swing for me personally. Matt's support was incredibly helpful to my psyche at the time. He rolled high in persuasion to make me feel like our plan would be a success. I tried to do the same for what his company was launching, and Matt told me how my support was the thing that lifted Beadle & Grimm's up when they were nervous no one would buy their stuff. Lifting each other up works both ways!

Then in 2020, when everyone was in the throes of quarantine and nervous breakdowns, Matt came on *Dragon Talk* again to help get people psyched up for D&D Live 2020 in early June. We were forced to hold the event completely virtually, which was a challenge on multiple levels, but Matt was super helpful in recruiting some of the actors and comedians who appeared in that show and supporting our efforts. He talked about what it's like to play D&D using video conferences as he made the foray into running a game, using digital images, using audio through Syrinscape,[2] and understanding that the energy needed to play D&D games online is very different than in person.

The thing that struck me the most from speaking with Matt so many times on the podcast and getting to know him offline over the years is that he is as much a part of the D&D community and fandom as anyone else. He comes off as a D&D nerd who just happens to have appeared in dozens of movies and TV projects. Meaning, Matt doesn't care about all that when he's rolling dice with his pals or hosting Twitch streams with his company. He gets what makes this game special on a visceral level. He cares about bringing *Dungeons & Dragons* to more people, and he's put his money where his mouth is. He's personally invested in making this game accessible for DMs with all the cool artifacts and tools in the editions of D&D adventures Beadle & Grimm's now publishes. He's incredibly gracious as an ambassador for D&D in the press, and he makes sure to be involved with charity drives and our live events as much as he can.

He's also a born performer who never fails to make me laugh with his good-natured, over-the-top persona. I'll take an off-the-rails interview with Matt any day of the week. I'm just happy to go along for the ride.

---

2. Greg: Syrinscape is an application that acts as a soundboard for Dungeon Masters so they can cue up music and sound effects to go along with what's happening in the game.

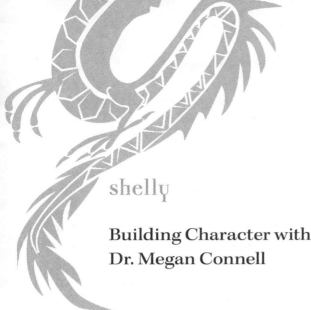

Building Character with
Dr. Megan Connell

My pediatrician when I was young seemed to be 183 years old. He was a short, squished-up, rosy-cheeked, mostly bald man with freckles the size of nickels dotting his scalp. I may have formed a stereotype of doctors thanks to good old Dr. Greene. Doctors were serious. They were highly intelligent. They were the very definition of "with age comes wisdom." Good doctors gave out lollipops—bonus points for the ones with the double paper sticks.

Now that I'm the age ol' Dr. Greene probably was when we met, I'm shocked at how young doctors actually are. (Same goes with librarians. When did they get so young? And wow, do they like to party!) As a kid it would be unfathomable to imagine Dr. Greene doing normal people things like grocery shopping, driving a car, or playing a game. Especially *Dungeons & Dragons*. Well, young Shelly, prepare to have your mind blown.

Dr. Megan Connell is a clinical psychologist and therapeutic Dungeon Master. She gave herself that title, and it's not as uncommon as you might think. I mean, all Dungeon Masters are kind of therapeutic in the same way hairdressers and Trader Joe's cashiers are. They are in a sense guiding you (your character) through (often) difficult paths and promise to give you a full refund if you don't like the crispy crunchy okra they recommended.

Megan started playing D&D when she was in middle school in 1993. She credits D&D with providing some of her best memories—hanging out with friends, telling stories, and making up characters. She stopped playing sometime after high school but got back into it after watching Wil Wheaton's *Ashes of Valkana* series on Geek & Sundry. Playing was still fun and great memories were already made, but as an adult and therapist, she noticed something else: D&D could provide numerous therapeutic benefits.

"You can't help but have your own 'stuff' seep into your character if you play them long enough," she said.

It got me thinking about my "stuff" and what my characters were trying to tell me. Astrid was my first D&D character. She was an elf sorceress who loved dogs, Boots of Speed, her friends, and hosting parties. She was intrigued by the idea of combat but preferred to spectate, lobbing *fireballs* and casting *dancing lights* from afar. Tabitha was my next long-term character. I wanted her to be different from Astrid because I felt like I shielded Astrid too much and didn't let her gain enough experience. Tabitha was a surly tiefling wizard, bit of a loner, may or may not have had made a pact with a demon (she definitely did), and traveled with a former circus show bear she rescued, named Oso de la Fez half the party pretended they couldn't see.[1] Both of these characters tended to hang in the background, and even though they got an A+ in charisma, they were awkward, shy, and disengaged in social situations. That's not me in real life, but in the game, I think I deliberately made this personality choice for three reasons:

1. I don't want to negotiate, disarm, seek information, charm, or answer questions because I (the real Shelly) am insecure in my rules and lore knowledge and don't want to screw things up for the party.
2. I do that crap in real life all the time and just want someone else to take care of business once in a while.
3. I'm afraid I'll get made fun of because I said or did something wrong. Do we ever outgrow that fear?

Even doctors have their own issues to work out, and Dr. Megan was no exception. D&D made all of it rise to the surface and if it happened for her, surely it was happening for other people. She knew she had to find a way to use the game in therapy.

A couple years earlier, Greg and I had the pleasure of interviewing Dr. Raffael Boccamazzo, a therapist who has used D&D to help children on the autism spectrum gain social skills. Dr. Megan came across the interview and was inspired. So really, Greg and I are pretty much doctors. Fortunately, the practice where Megan worked was all for innovation and trying out new

---

1. Shelly: Fun fact: Oso de la Fez has been statted up to be one of the most overpowered familiars in D&D history! Google him.

tactics, so they were on board with incorporating a little dice rolling into therapy sessions.

At the time of the interview, Dr. Megan ran two therapeutic D&D groups a week (with hopes of adding more). The first group was focused on teaching social skills with archfey. Turns out these god-like fey beings are pretty good teachers. Dr. Megan introduced the group to one archfey after another, forcing them to key into the norms of this court. Did they pick up on the nonverbal social cues? What's the hierarchy? What does this archfey like and dislike? Most of the kids were on the autism spectrum and might find it difficult to pick up on these things.

Upon returning to town after a quick jaunt to the Shadowfell,[2] the group immediately wanted to trade in all their used equipment and go for an upgrade. Dr. Megan told them they could certainly try but wanted to know how their characters would feel in this moment. They're tired, having just returned from probable battle on a plane full of ick and death and despair, now in a town full of strangers, missing the homes they hadn't seen in six months. What would it feel like for them to walk into this village? Were darksteel greatswords really a top priority? That's when it clicked for at least one of the party members. Choices shouldn't be driven by the desires of the player. He was able to put himself into his character's mind, feel a little (safely) freaked out, and encourage the party to check into the local inn to regroup and find some normalcy. There's no meta-gaming in this group! They help each other when they notice someone struggling. And that's how you develop empathy.

One group was comprised of all girls because Dr. Megan felt like there just weren't enough young women who game. Under her Dungeon Mastering, these girls learned empowerment, leadership, and how to say no. Let that sink in for a moment, because it's one of the greatest things I've ever heard about D&D (right up there with the tiefling wizard and her rescued circus bear familiar).

"D&D is 'pretend play' with more structure," Dr. Megan noted.

The girls in this group ranged in age from thirteen to eighteen and were all new to D&D. Like most of us, they started off playing characters who closely resembled how they saw themselves or wanted to be seen.

"We either play the direct opposite of ourselves or the aspirational self," Dr. Megan said. (*See* Astrid and Tabitha.)

---

2. Shelly: A bleak, desolate, plane full of misery and decay. Definitely send your kids there. Good times!

Encountering difficult people or situations in game allows the group to practice before facing them in real life. Were the girls dubious about what Dr. Megan was asking them to do? Probably. But if my doctor told me to sit down, pick up an imaginary sword, and play a game for two hours while my mom sat in the waiting room reading back issues of *Redbook* magazine, I'd be like, "no idea what my parents think is happening in here, but let's hope they don't find out!"

Saying no was awkward. I went on dates with guys I wasn't interested in and then ghosted them at a bar three hours later because that was easier than declining their invitation in the first place. I let friends borrow sentimental things because it was easier than explaining why I didn't want to part with it. Once I got booted from a volunteer group that went around to high schools and roleplayed scenarios about drugs and sex and peer pressure to teach kids how to stand up for themselves (the irony) because the director said I never told her about an upcoming vacation. I did. I know I did. And I just sat there like, "Oh, okay. Sorry about that." In hindsight it was a totally dorky job so maybe it was a good thing I got fired, but I'm still angry all these years later that I didn't have the nerve to graciously let her know she had made a mistake.

What Dr. Megan is teaching these girls is life-changing. Some people never master that skill. And if D&D can do that, it should be required for the youth. But there's even more going on here with this group of girls. Age thirteen is the height of competitiveness among girls, and it starts well before then. I saw that at my son's daycare as early as four years old. The boys were quietly building ramps for their Hot Wheels and the girls were deciding which one of them wasn't allowed to be in their make-believe classroom. For "pretend play," the hurt was very real for the little girl left out. One of the best skills kids can learn is how to be a good friend and the value of maintaining friendships. My girlfriends are more important to me now than they ever were. The need to look out for each other, build each other up, celebrate each other's successes and differences, and oh look—I'm describing a D&D party again. Empowerment and learning to say no doesn't have to come at the expense of your female allies. It's in support of them. Where was Dr. Megan when I was thirteen? Oh right, not born yet.

Back to the awesome girl group. Before heading into potentially problematic territory, Dr. Megan talked about it with the group to prepare them. They also used X cards, which allow players to immediately opt out of content or situations in a game that are uncomfortable by tapping or holding the card.

No questions asked. The Dungeon Master simply moves on. TRPGs (tabletop roleplaying games) by their nature are improvisational, so you don't always know the direction the story will take.[3]

The role of party leader naturally rotates around the table. Sharing the spotlight happens naturally—another thing atypical for girls this age. Sometimes Dr. Megan's colleagues will join the group as NPCs. One played a character who was trapped in a toxic relationship where she was forced to give up her family and friends. The players had to find a way to get through to this character so she could see the damage her relationship was causing. Eventually the boyfriend revealed himself to be a black dragon, and the party had to fight him to save the NPC. They emerged victorious in combat, but perhaps the real win was what they learned about relationships. It took two weeks in game for the girls to build enough trust with this NPC to get her to admit she needed her friends and family. They could see how easy it was to fall into a bad relationship, miss or disregard all the red flags, and learn what to look for before it was too late. Some people never learn this skill. The therapist who played the NPC specialized in abusive relationships and is now also an advocate for D&D and therapy.

Every week Dr. Megan sent an email to parents letting them know how the sessions went, strengths and weaknesses, and what they may want to follow up on with their kids. Parents had every reason to be on board, regardless of their D&D knowledge. Some noticed significant changes after only a few sessions. One father told Dr. Megan he saw a difference in the way his daughter interacted with her school friends and her D&D friends. The school friends were competitive and petty. The D&D friends were supportive and inclusive. Guess which ones will stick around?

One of the biggest D&D-as-therapy success stories for Dr. Megan was watching the kids develop a whole new approach to problem solving. Maybe those cultists were under the influence of mind-flayers and can't control their actions. Maybe the bad guy is a bully because he's being bullied. Dr. Megan has seen whole sessions dedicated to healing opponents instead of trying to get to the boss monster or treasure. I'm going to approach bad guys differently now. Maybe in real life too.

Roleplaying isn't new to therapy. It's a tool that has been around for years.

---

3. Shelly: John Stavropoulos has a great document with tons of safety tools to reference. https://tinyurl.com/ycyava86. Follow @TTRPGSafetyKit on Twitter for more support tools curated by Kienna Shaw and Lauren Bryant-Monk.

Thanks to the work of therapists like Dr. B. and Dr. Megan, there's a whole network of therapists incorporating D&D into their practices.

Speaking of practices, Dr. Megan practices what she, well, practices. She's part of a weekly D&D stream called *Clinical Role* comprised of other therapists, including Dr. B.

"Therapists are notoriously bad at self-care," she noted. D&D is how they relax, recharge, and work on themselves for a bit.

Sometimes you can't see what's happening in your own life until you see it literally played out before you. Once Greg played a half-elf with a backstory he kind of cobbled together on the fly. His dad left. His mom was a human of "ill repute." She left too. He never really thought much of the backstory until over time the Dungeon Master would weave these characters into the story giving Greg a chance to interact with them.

"Wow," the DM said to Greg. "You have a lot of issues we're working on right now." It was a bit eye-opening. *Did* he have issues he needed to work through with his own parents?

"Granted, the Dungeon Master was a pothead from New York and not a clinical psychologist," Greg admitted. But still.

Who knows where it could have gone? It's interesting to think of D&D as holding up a mirror. You get to "star in your own salvation" as Dr. Megan would say. It's easier to fight your demons when you're surrounded by your friends. *Fireballs* and a Holy Avenger help too.

I asked Dr. Megan if she noticed a difference in play styles between boys and girls.

> "Girls are more likely to interact with the world," she explained. "They love social encounters. Once, they spent an entire session shopping for ball gowns. Boys tend to want to kill something."
>
> Greg would like the record to show he also likes shopping sessions.
>
> Shopping in Dr. Megan's game would be especially entertaining when you pursue the goods at places like Blood, Bath, and Beyond and REI (Rogues, Elves, and Imps).

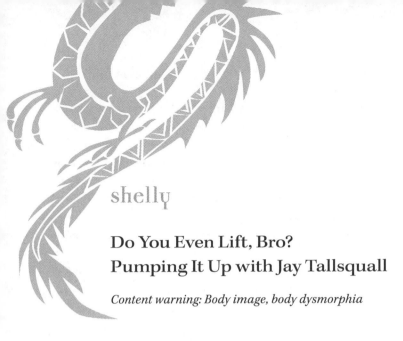

Do You Even Lift, Bro?
Pumping It Up with Jay Tallsquall

Content warning: Body image, body dysmorphia

I volunteered once at my kid's school and got to spend recess with him. Here's what I learned from my field research:

- Kids these days don't care if you're an adult. If you're on the blacktop your face is fair game for a kickball. Also, it's fun to hit adults in the face with kickballs. Especially if they're really screamy about it.
- Kids have a lot of stamina.
- Your own child will turn against you and pretend not to know you when other kids are hitting you in the face with kickballs.
- Kids don't know they're exercising if they're doing something enjoyable like pelting adults with kickballs.

Similar to the wily ways in which D&D sneaks math, reading, and writing into kids' lives, monkey bars, tag, and riding bikes burn calories, build endurance, and all that other healthy stuff kids don't realize is happening. They're not chasing adults off a playground because they're concerned about their BMI or fitting into a dress before their best friend's wedding. They're doing it because it's fun.

Wait, *what*? Fun?

I have spent a lot of time in gyms slogging through workouts I didn't enjoy because I did enjoy beer, cheese, and bread. As a parent, I have also spent a lot of time at playgrounds. Once when my son and I were the only ones at the park, I felt emboldened enough to try my hand at the ol' monkey bars and promptly fell six feet into a pile of soggy bark chips. My quads burned for three days after two and a half minutes on the teeter-totter. My son told me I was the worst tag player ever because it's no fun to tag someone who kept tripping over their own ankles and was always on the verge of barfing from exhaustion. My child can literally run circles around me and not because he's in better shape. (Okay, it totally is.) But it's also because for him, it's not a workout. It's play. When did exercise stop being fun?

Tabletop gaming is fun but is generally a sedentary activity that often involves snacks and beverages (mmmm, beer, cheese, and bread . . .). Gamers aren't predisposed to unhealthy BMIs, but adults are. This "fact" is brought to you by my bitterness at watching my metabolism drop faster than a wizard's hit points after a tarrasque attack. I'm no scientist, but ten years ago I could eat a wheel of brie in one sitting without consequences. Adults are busy—kids, jobs, family, and trying to make sure the invasive weeds in your yard don't choke out the pine bonsai tree in your neighbor's yard. When you have free time, you want to spend it with friends or hobbies or lying prone on the couch bathed in the pixels of your favorite show. Let's leave lifting heavy axes and traipsing through uncharted terrain to our player characters. We'll handle the long rests. Besides, ancient lore states that geeks don't work out. I mean, unless you LARP.[1]

Perhaps we need some inspiration, and not just the kind your Dungeon Master can dole out as a reward for playing your character true to their nature. For me, inspiration came in the form of a hashtag.

I can't remember when I first stumbled down the #DnDFitness rabbit hole, but as I wound my way through the sweat-soaked Spandex-clad warrens, I discovered a subculture of the D&D community I didn't know existed. It's no secret the people in our community are often each other's biggest fans. They marvel at each other's cosplay, they appear as guests on each other's streams, they play and rave about each other's design work. But this was celebrating something totally different. I found a world in which fellow gamers posted about their workouts to the acclaim and admiration of strangers. There was no critiquing of form, body shaming, or thirsty elitism. It was simply a network of people bound together by their love of D&D who genuinely wanted to send encouraging words to strangers. I had to find out who was responsible

---

1. Shelly: LARP is an acronym that stands for live action roleplaying, where the players physically portray their characters.

for this, so I launched a years-long forensic cyber-investigation. Just kidding! I asked Greg.

"Oh, that's Jay Tallsquall," he said.

Fortunately, Greg keeps his finger on the pulse of the D&D community and had been following Jay for years. Jay was a D&D streamer, cosplayer, and fitness guru, and he has one of the coolest last names ever. He said Googling him will either net you a Land's End squall jacket available in tall sizes or the man responsible for unleashing a fitness movement for the D&D world.

We interviewed Jay over Zoom and even through my smudgy, dusty computer screen, his kind eyes and big smile lit up the room. He sported a bright purple beard, which held more significance than just being a cool fashion choice.

If you saw Jay in the gym, you might think he's someone people pay to yell at them while he increased the incline on their treadmill, but he's not. He's a compassionate, empathetic dude who has struggled with body dysmorphia for years and is here to help people live their best lives. He came to D&D like many—through popular shows like *Critical Role*—and has been an active member of the community. As a streamer, he not only Dungeon Mastered for *Vice*, a campaign that lasted 140 sessions, he also helped raise nearly $20,000 for eighteen different charities. Like so many who spend giant chunks of their lives trying to belong, he finally found that home in D&D.

About that brightly colored facial hair. Jay identifies as asexual (ace) and is a proud member of the LGBTQIA+ communities. Purple doesn't just represent ace pride, it means that Jay had finally found acceptance in his sexual orientation. Part of Jay's mission is education and representation, so he graciously broke it down for us. Asexuality is an umbrella term that exists as a spectrum. Asexual people do not experience sexual attraction in the way most people do, but they do crave intimacy and deep emotional connections. For years Jay wondered if he was broken because he didn't fit the perceived normative profile. All men think about is sex, right? So what happens if you're a man who doesn't think about sex. Like at all. You'll probably default to assuming something is wrong with you. Every time well-meaning friends and family would recite "You just haven't found the right person yet," it was another nail closing the lid of a box Jay would never fit into.

Thankfully, he had D&D, a place he returned to often when seeking solace. Storytelling was in his DNA. Growing up, Jay was an avid reader and plowed through all the Dragonlance books. He had big family reunions culminating with everyone around a campfire taking turns making up a story and passing it along. Jay's love for narration and world-building was fanned like the embers at the center of these memories. He loved having a way to gamify stories and being the hero when you felt like anything but.

Around the age of thirty, Jay discovered weightlifting. In a way it was wish fulfillment—a way to bring some of those big, strong characters he heroically played in D&D to his real life.

Finding out about asexuality was a huge relief for him. All those years wondering what was wrong fit into place now that he could quite literally define himself. He had a community and people to reach out and talk to. At Gen Con 2018, the always popular and largest tabletop gaming convention in North America, Jay officially came out and wore his colors in public for the first time. He credited the influence of the D&D community with how he was able to get to this pivotal moment in his life.

A little about attending Gen Con if you haven't experienced it. The first one I went to was in 1999, a couple of months after I started at Wizards. I had no idea what to expect, how to use traveler's checks, or even where Milwaukee was on a map (because honestly, the Midwest is just confusing. It isn't that far west when you're from the East Coast, okay?), but I was a super eager new Wizard and all of my new friends were going. Before Gen Con, my convention attendance was limited to a gift basket trade show in Scranton, Pennsylvania, and a psychic fair at the West Palm Beach Airport Marriott. Gen Con was not like either.

By day I dined on crappy convention center food, which for a vegetarian meant jumbo pretzels, bagels, and blueberry muffins. Evenings I hung out with coworkers at a spy-themed bar called the Safe House, where if you didn't know the password to gain entry, they would broadcast you standing outside doing something embarrassing to the whole bar. Super stressful.

What struck me the most about Gen Con was the inclusive vibe. You could almost hear the sound of guards being let down. Here you could be yourself, fly your freakiest flag. Nerd Nirvana. No judgment, no stigmas, no risk of being made fun of or bullied. Gen Con was a place where everyone fit in, united by a passion for the geekiest of hobbies. Talk about a safe house.

Buoyed by the energy and vocal support of Gen Con, Jay took to Twitter to talk about his experience and connect with others who felt different. It clicked for them, the way it had for Jay, and he realized how important it was to have good representation for the ace community—a mantle he took upon himself.

A common narrative we hear on *Dragon Talk* is how D&D allows players to safely explore self-identity or what it's like to walk a mile on difficult terrain in someone else's Boots of Speed. For a game steeped in fantasy, the impact it can have on real life is staggering. A woman discovers the truth about her sexual orientation. A man comes to grips with past trauma. A teenager feels what it's like to be in control for the first time. There's a reason therapists have been using roleplaying tactics for decades.

Firmly embedded in the D&D world, Jay became known for cosplay and fitness. If you saw Jay "getting swole" at your local Planet Fitness you'd probably assume he was laughing at your noodle arms and never approach him for advice. But we know better than to make snap judgments based on someone's appearance. Jay is the least judgmental person you'll meet in a gym. He would probably be dressed like Shazam, which makes him a lot more welcoming.

With his nice guy reputation preceding him, people started asking advice about embarking on their own fitness journeys. As much as he was inspiring these online strangers, they were inspiring him. Soon, his two passions collided and a huge, momentous community effort and the uplifting hashtag #DnDFitness were born.

Jay went beyond doling out advice. He became a virtual trainer, starting with challenges like Magic Missile Push-Ups where participants rolled a d4 and did that many push-ups over the course of the day. People loved it! Soon the hashtag was flooded with videos of people doing their push-ups. More themed challenges followed, more polyhedral dice were rolled, more lives were changed for the better. Jay was reframing how people viewed working out. Boring, laborious pull-ups became your character pulling themselves out of a well.

Wanting this to become a true community effort, Jay encouraged fans to submit their own #DnDFitness challenges. The hashtag grew beyond creative exercises into a place where followers shared successes, broke through obstacles, and gained moral support.

I like searching the hashtag when I should be out for a jog or doing some crunches (not rage-eating the boxed mac and cheese my son claimed was "too cheesy") because we all need some feel-good stories. There are thousands of people following #DnDFitness who may never know the impetus or the person behind it, and as long as they're inspired by it, that's totally okay with Jay. So to answer my titular question, yeah, he lifts, bro. He lifts hearts and minds and he's barely breaking a sweat.

I couldn't help but wonder how my D&D character stayed fit. Were *fireballs* heavy? Did the quarantine fifteen make levitation a bit harder? Could she use her spell books for ankle raises? Sure, all characters probably have no trouble meeting their daily step goal when it's an exploration day, but if she wants to cast *shocking grasp* without taking a sickly gasp, elevating the heart rate is key. We asked Jay for the ideal exercises for some of D&D's most popular classes. Here's what we came up with:

Rogues: Planks because they need good core strength to sneak under things.

Magic users: "Conducting" movements to strengthen shoulder and arm muscles, key for spell casting.

Paladins: Pull-ups because they're a good all-around workout and also we love alliteration.

Clerics: Farmer carries because they're always lugging unconscious bodies around.

Barbarians: Kettlebells. Feels obvious.

Monks: Battle ropes, which require strength and dexterity.

Artificers: Flipping monster truck tires to build stamina for moving big parts and pieces for their various contraptions.

Greg

Kade Wells Teaches Us
How to Be Better Students

Teacher of Wizards. That's the phrase that comes to mind when I think of Kade Wells. Well, that and Morgan Freeman in *Lean on Me*. But mostly I'm in awe of what he accomplished as a teacher, educator, and mentor to kids in early high school in the least privileged parts of Houston, Texas. Frustrated while trying to teach for several years and not getting through, Kade realized something about himself. He grew up on a farm in South Dakota, and was a relatively well read and intelligent learner, furthered because he played D&D in his adolescent years. He thought the best way to encourage his students—many of whom were absolutely resistant to any kind of (*gasp*) reading—was to introduce inner-city kids to the magic of *Dungeons & Dragons*. And not just in the hey-why-don't-you-join-an-after-school-club kind of way. Kade put D&D directly in his classroom on the first day of school.

"Kids just simply don't read anymore," Kade told us when we first talked to him in October 2015. He said he worked in a Title I high school and those dang video games and other digital distractions prevented most kids from ever wanting to pick up a book. He really painted a dire picture of how teenagers are lacking basic skills and worse, the desire to improve those skills.

"These days kids have a cell phone in their pocket that's connected to games on the internet and everything is spoon-fed to them," he said. "So in ninth grade, when they really have to become real people, they have to start showing research capabilities and analytical capabilities and their writing has to be on the way to getting them into college. And none of them are ready."

Then Kade had his brilliant idea—what if they *weren't* real people at all?!

What if they *pretended* to be real people in a game? What if he used the fun of D&D as a carrot for getting these kids to use these skills instead of the teacher yelling at them to open a dang book?

"I realized that *Dungeons & Dragons* was primarily responsible for the intelligence I now possess," he said.

What exactly did D&D teach him? "The ability to think, truly," Kade said. "Since the core mechanic is to create a 'life,' you can use it to teach just about anything. Morality. All the things that go with it. Math. Reading. Communication. Maps. It's all there. It's one of the most impressive cross-curriculum tools I have ever seen."

He started with the D&D club route, where interested kids would meet up after school to play with each other under Kade's direction. Just doing that yielded some really great results in teaching kids cognitive skills without them knowing they were learning said cognitive skills. But the real aha! moment occurred when he took students who normally aren't thought of as the target demographic for D&D, like football players.

"I had eighteen football players in my tutorial today," Kade told us.[1] He split them up into teams, worked with them to create D&D characters, and ran a deathmatch combat with their characters where the team who survived the fray was declared the winner. "They were so excited! . . . But the point is: eighteen football players diligently sat, rolling dice, looking at the characters, flipping through the spells in the book to find what their character was going to do in any one moment, and I smiled. Because some of these kids seemingly had never seen a book before."

"We basically had D&D boot camp," he said, and the immediate results were extraordinary. Kade described how they were suddenly using all the skills he would normally have to painstakingly teach using outdated characters like Dick and Jane instead of Elric and Chardan the Bold. The football players were looking in the table of contents and indexes to find the information they needed. They were scanning the page to find the details they needed, looking at headings, and using logic to choose the spells and abilities to complement their teammates.

---

1. Greg: In this interview I learned that a tutorial is a forced session of learning meant for a student to stave off failing a class and becoming ineligible to play a sport. Football coaches have a lot of sway in the American South, if the advertising around *Friday Night Lights* is to be believed.

"They were doing all the things as an English teacher we want them to do, but the point is they were doing it intrinsically," Kade said. "They're doing it for their own sake because they want to succeed in the game. That's what I realized was so valuable about using *Dungeons & Dragons* as a teaching tool."

It worked! His kids tested 9.4 percent higher than the district average! The students who played D&D with Kade were more successful in high school. Full stop. They took tests better, they scored higher, and they chose behaviors that helped them learn better simply because they learned those skills playing D&D. Here's the really striking thing: the results didn't just affect the kids in the club. The skills absorbed by kids in the D&D club contributed to scores going up in the general student population. The entire class learned better. That's remarkable! The research proved that playing D&D really made students, well, smarter.

Kade took his lived experience as a teacher and his on-the-job research using D&D to motivate students and created a cohesive snapshot of his findings with two researchers from Sam Houston University. He went to the World Literacy Conference in Klagenfurt, Austria, in July 2015 to present what he had figured out in Texas. The group of administrators from around the world were impressed with the results of Kade's symposium. As an aside, I definitely got a kick out of picturing Kade Wells, bald South Dakotan farm boy with an overly polite mode of speech full of "yes, ma'ams" and "yes, sirs," presenting to a group of stuffy Europeans wearing powdered wigs that they should all start playing D&D in the classroom. Talk about a slam dunk!

Based on the response to his presentation in Austria, Kade went whole hog that September when school started. "I decided to really go for it," he said. "The research that I presented in Klagenfurt dictates that this is a tool that works." So he figured it was probably better to integrate D&D into everyday classroom activity. Why leave all the benefits only to the students who signed up for the D&D club? "I want to make every kid smarter, not just the smart kids smarter. Smart kids are already smart!"

On the first day of school, he had every kid in his English class roll up D&D characters using the *Player's Handbook*.[2] The avatar they made became their persona for the whole year. It makes classroom management a little easier because D&D has an experience point system that he can use to give rewards for good behavior or remove for bad actions. Beyond that, he has figured out

2. Greg: Probably the most used of the core rulebooks for D&D.

that D&D makes teaching things like interpreting text easier to understand when placing the student in the story. Kade has always found the staid descriptions of most situations in the standard texts to be boring. It comes to life when presented in the framework of D&D.

He gave an example. "The first adventure is called 'On the Road' and it's a mood-based piece. Mood is one of our standards. Kids have to be able to pull the mood out of a piece of text and identify what the mood is," he said. "On the adventure [in the classroom], I'm directly addressing them. It's different than when the text reads, 'Shirley was walking down the road and she saw a balloon floating in the sky.' The kids cannot connect to that. But when I say, 'You are walking along the road, and the rain is dripping down your collar, the mud is squishing under your boots, and you smell the decay coming from the cemetery.' There is a buy-in there that the kids have because you are directly addressing them and they have this identity with the characters they've made."

"I'm crossing the game mechanics directly with the school instruction," Kade said.

If that sounds like a much cooler way to experience education than most of what went on in your high school, you are not alone. What Kade talked about in this interview in 2015 seemed to ignite a trend among educators, including an instructor named Sarah Roman who taught at a private school in New Jersey. She began using D&D in her classroom, teaching English in a different way than Kade by having the students go on a semester-long campaign to save Britain through a series of adventures she wrote. Sarah taught English literature to honors students by creating adventures that mirrored the plot of the books the kids had to read. Their adventurers fought Grendel's mother, a humanoid beast from the epic poem *Beowulf,* and eventually contended against each other in a *Lord of the Flies*–style adventure where the students were shipwrecked on an abandoned island.

Shelly and I spoke with Kade and Sarah about their approaches to using D&D in the classroom in 2018. I had privately kept up correspondence with Kade and encouraged him to reach out to other teachers to codify some of what they were doing in combining classroom instruction with *Dungeons & Dragons.* One person saving the education system wasn't going to work, no matter what *Lean on Me* had to say about it. The goal was to build up a critical mass of teachers around the world and perhaps develop a curriculum or product that could be sold to school districts and help revolutionize how we approach teaching, especially when it came to kids from less privileged areas.

A lot has changed in the education realm as I type this in 2021—you may have heard about D&D helping people get together on Zoom and stay in touch with friends and family during quarantine. But there is less energy being spent to revolutionize the classroom when thinking about kids in the same physical room around a table playing D&D makes me think about virus transmission, not the Wizard School of Transmutation. Do you realize how many germs might be on those dice?!

That said, I hope humans as a society get back thinking about how more games like D&D in the classroom can help make learning fun and exciting for kids. Beyond all the evidence we discussed, the most important aspect to me is how playing D&D can improve the soft skills of students. The game doesn't just make you a better learner. I'd go so far as to say that it makes you a better person.

Sarah and Kade gave really great examples of this happening to their students. "One time during observation, my supervisor was in there watching my students do a group lesson," Sarah told us. They weren't playing D&D that day, but the supervisor remarked that it was incredible to see so many of the students helping each other out in order to get through the assignment "for the greater good." Sounds like an alignment, doesn't it?

"One of [the supervisor's] comments was, 'I don't know how you've gotten them to talk to each other like this. Because the collaboration level was so rich. They feel comfortable with each other. They feel skilled. They know what the other is working toward.' That's all earned through play," Sarah said, chalking up that rich collaboration to the type of cooperation they had to use while playing D&D in the classroom.

After all, it takes a village to kill Grendel.

Kade's story was a real tear-jerker. "A couple years ago there was this great sweet kid named Jimmy, and Jimmy was probably one of the smartest kids in the school," he said. "He was just isolated. He was crying in the middle of the hallway one day, and I came up to him—he wasn't one of my students, but I was like, 'Little brother, you okay?' and he says, 'Mister, I'm just so alone. Everybody here is so different.'"

"And he was right, they were very different than him," Kade said with a little laugh. "He was a shining star in a field of darkness. I told him, 'You are going to join my D&D club. And I'm going to have you moved into my classroom.' Both of those things happened. I told the administrator this kid needs to be in my room."

Jimmy started playing D&D with Kade and joined his class before moving on to have a successful high school career. Jimmy is now a senior, and he wrote Kade a letter and sent it to him through the mail at school.

"Jimmy wrote me a three-page letter explaining how everything that had happened after that moment I found him in the hallway changed his life for the better," Kade said.

That one moment of kindness and action from Kade changed this kid's life. It's like some prophecy out of a fantasy novel. "Now he's going to be an engineer when he leaves school. And he still plays with the D&D group."

Shelly and I had literal tears in our eyes listening to this story.[3] It's so sweet to hear how D&D and a dedicated mentor can have such a positive effect on the lives of struggling kids. Maybe writing papers or doing trigonometry proofs wouldn't be such a pain in the butt if you imagined your character, the brilliant wizard Montalero, was doing your homework instead.

---

3. Greg: "Shut it down!" Shelly quipped. "No one can see us like this!" There's a reason we don't call the podcast *Dragon Cry*. It would ruin our image. Hoda and Kathie Lee never cried like that!

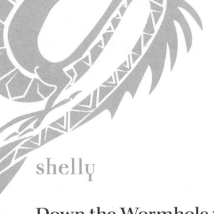

Down the Wormhole with Emily Axford

One night Bart and I were scrolling through our thirteen thousand streaming services complaining about having nothing to watch. It was looking like another evening watching American expats complain about rustic wood accents and tiny appliances on *House Hunters International* when a thumbnail on the screen caught my eye.

"What's that?" I asked Bart.

"*Hot Date*? Never heard of it."

"Me either, but it's my new favorite show."

I have excellent instincts when it comes to quality TV shows. It's basically my superpower. I know Greg will read this and say, "But you watch *The Bachelor*!" Chill, Greg. While that is true, there is a whole side of my entertainment-watching habits you don't know about. I'm classy sometimes.

Three hours later, Bart and I had binged the entire first season of *Hot Date*. Once again, my instincts proved right.

If you haven't seen it yet, here's the elevator pitch: *Hot Date* is a comedy series about modern-day relationships starring Emily Axford and Brian K. Murphy, who play multiple roles, each slightly more absurd yet relatable than the next. If you're intrigued, I grant you permission to put down this book, watch it, and come back so you'll have even more appreciation for our super-fun interview with Emily.

First, a little context: I've been majorly starstruck twice. The first was in fifth grade when my mom took me to see early 1980s soft rock super-duo Air Supply in concert. On the way home, a limo sidled up next to us, the window rolled down, and the two gentlemen from the band were staring into the passenger side of my mom's green Cordoba.

"*Oh my God!*" my mom screamed. "It's *them*! Roll down your window! *Say something*!"

Now, you may be thinking, "My mom took me to an Air Supply concert" is perhaps the most uncool sentence ever written. You are correct, but stay with me. I did not roll down my window or smile and wave. I stared straight ahead and ignored the three people I loved the most.

The second time my starstruck-ness was anticipatory when I found out Emily was going to be a guest on *Dragon Talk*.

Who is Emily Axford, and why is she one of my most favorite people? She's a supremely talented writer, actress, and producer who happens to be a D&D aficionado. After my hot date binging *Hot Date*, I felt like I had a new best friend and imagined all the fun things we would get up to. Join book clubs for the sole purpose of seeing other people's living rooms and drinking boxed wine. Themed Halloween costumes. BE FRI and ST ENDS tattoos. Did any of these things seem more plausible than spending an afternoon at work chatting with Emily and bonding over our favorite geeky hobby? I have learned to expect the unexpected when it comes to D&D.

One day, I noticed Brian "Murph" Murphy on the list of upcoming guests and knew the name was familiar, but it's a pretty common name. There are probably three Brian Murphys within three blocks of where you are right now. After reading his bio, it clicked who this Brian Murphy was, none other than Dungeon Master for *Not Another D&D Podcast* (or *NADDPOD* if you're cool and a fan). I was neither of those things yet (one of those I'm still not) even though everyone I knew worshipped *NADDPOD*. Like bowed down to the mighty NADDs. Err, okay that didn't come out right. I decided to amend my ways and see what the fuss was about.

About three seconds into the first episode, I realized why people love it. It's incredibly funny and clever, and I was already invested in the characters—especially the "Crick Elf," Moonshine Cybin. Then I was struck with a strong case of déjà vu. Did I already listen to this podcast? Do these people also do *Bachelor* recaps? Why was it so familiar? OMG, I knew those voices! This was Brian and Emily from *Hot Date* and OMG, they play D&D![1] Did we just become best friends?

---

1. Shelly: It seems only natural to have D&D and *Hot Date* crossover, right? Get this—there almost was! Emily and Murph wrote an episode, but the TV execs (much like *Seattle Times* editors) didn't get it, so it was rewritten to be about *Werewolf* instead. A *very* funny episode regardless.

If you're a fan of *NADDPOD* (and okay let's be honest, you probably are), it will be no surprise that Murph was an absolutely delightful guest, and I held it together until the end of the interview when I mentioned I may be Emily's biggest fan.

"Oh, she's right in the next room!" Murph noted, and I pretty much hit the floor.

Once I regained my composure (seventeen days later), I suggested Emily as a potential guest and immediately regretted it. How good is an interview if one of the hosts just sits there looking like a big, dumb ten-year-old in a green Cordoba? To my surprise, she said yes, and a couple months later Greg and I were talking to Emily about her "lusty" foray into the world of D&D.

A night of *Call of Cthulhu*, the horror-themed roleplaying game, triggered the realization for Emily that roleplaying games were fun.

"You hang out with friends, being you, but also sillier, more awesome versions of you," she remembered.

Knowing not much more than that D&D was a thing, she immediately went on the lookout for a Dungeon Master. I loved this visual. How does one "look out" for a Dungeon Master? Are they sitting at Starbucks, hunched behind a screen, sipping a trenta iced coffee? Can you see the outline of a d20 in their back pocket? When asked for directions do they furiously rub their hands together and ask if you *really* want to go there?[2]

At a party, Emily overheard her friend and beloved Dungeon Master for *Dimension 20* (and former *Dragon Talk* guest) Brennan Lee Mulligan mention D&D. That was the opening she needed. He agreed to run a game for her, and the rest is comedy roleplaying gold history.

Now, I know what you're thinking. "Wow, Shelly, you and Emily have so much in common!" It's true! We're both from upstate New York. We both have dark hair and short-term memory issues. We played D&D 3.5 edition first. We both married guys with first names that begin with B. Basically we'd be the same person if not for one huge discrepancy.

Emily had a bad Dungeon Mastering experience and *liked* it. My bad experience has scarred me for life, but Emily's experience only made her hungry for more opportunities to DM. The failing made it fun!

I hope we can still be friends.

The major difference in our blundered DMing attempts was that Emily rec-

---

2. Greg: I have totally met this DM.

ognized all the ways she was "bad" and welcomed the opportunity to learn from them and do better next time.

Lessons learned:

1. Like a cool babysitter or friend's mom who just wants to party with you, she let players do whatever they wanted and kept giving them souped-up magic items. They wound up being too overpowered for the adventure she planned.
2. She created too big of a world for a short one-off. They only did a fraction of what she planned. This is like spending hours making mille-feuilles from scratch only to have your dinner party guests eat the store-bought cookies you put in your son's lunch instead. (Still bitter!)
3. She thinks it's actually kind of fun to suck at something.

Well, maybe if you don't already suck at lots of things it could be a novelty? "DM for me!" she said. "You'll like it! I want you to succeed!"

"But Emily," I said. "I almost couldn't *talk* to you. How could I be a DM?" In other words, let's change the subject, shall we?

"Do it," she commanded. "You'll feel better."

I swear I'm getting nervous writing this because I know what happens after. But it was so clever how she duped me into DMing. A real Jedi mind trick.

So Emily and Greg were talking about how the best Dungeon Masters were the ones who let the interests of the players help inform the story instead of getting all angsty and spiraling when the story doesn't go how it was planned. Yeah, yeah, yeah. I feel really seen, guys. Perhaps I looked a little defeated because Greg said, "Don't worry, Shelly. You'll get there."

Emily said, "Yeah! When I'm in your game, I'll ask if I can do a Perception check to see if there are any worm people here, you're going to be excited!"

Excited? By worm people? Eh. Maybe if the worm people were competing in a televised game show to win a husband. But I played along and explained that regardless of what she rolled, she had 100 percent confidence there were no worm people there. The end.

But she continued. "I do a Survival check to see if there are any worm people in these puddles . . . and roll a nat twenty!"[3]

---

3. Shelly: "Nat" is short for "natural" and "nat 20" means you rolled a twenty on the die naturally—no bonuses needed! If you roll a twenty on an attack roll, it's considered a critical hit.

Oh, okay. I saw what was happening here. Now there are puddles in this world? And Survival checks? And nat twenties? What's next? Black limousines filled with 1980s soft rock super duos? I did what any inexperienced DM would do.

"As you're bending over to get a closer look into the puddles, something grabs you around the neck and pulls you down!"

Oldest trick in the DM book. Except it backfired. She was intrigued by the wormhole she was being sucked into.

"I go limp and give in to the wormhole," she said.

And she had company.

"I kind of want to see what's down there too now," Greg said.

Greg!

"Do you want to save her?" I asked.

But Emily was no damsel in distress. She reached her hand out to Greg and invited him to follow her, an invitation he gleefully accepted.

"Okay, fine," I said. "You're both freefalling for . . . months." I figured that might buy me some time to figure out what came next.

"You're doing it!" Greg said like he was yelling after one of his daughters riding off without training wheels. "You're DMing!"

That was impossible! I hadn't broken a sweat or regretted all my life choices that led me to this moment. But okay. I let my two players tumble down a wormhole, maybe for all of eternity because I wasn't really sure what was down there either. Dare I say, I was feeling a bit inspired. I could already feel myself overpreparing for this adventure. I was going to be a Dungeon Master! For Emily, no less!

"By the way," Emily said. "We're 12th level. And multiclassed."

So sad what happened to Greg and Emily. They never saw those rocks coming.

greg

The Critical Power of Bards: Omega Jones

Society is a collaborative storytelling game.

That sounds better than just saying "society is a D&D game" for some reason, but it's the same idea. The point is that humanity's whole existence depends on individuals, on average, making choices that benefit the species as a whole. Lifting each other up isn't just important in the D&D community, it's important for society to function at all. That's why Omega Jones, aka the Critical Bard, stepped up to the mic in 2020. He saw something he could do to lift up the Black voices in this country when they were hurting by hosting conversations on his Twitch channel. Dubbed "Black AF Roundtables," he invited prominent voices in the D&D community to talk through their experiences and trauma following the death of George Floyd.[1] It was raw. There was anger and hurt on display, but there was also community in sharing those experiences, and the desire to get through it all together.

Kinda sounds like a D&D party, right?

Omega showed that there was value in communicating the reality of being a Black person who loved to play this game. It is not all arias and uplifting refrains—the racist power structures in place in our society are frankly still as apparent for some at the gaming table as they are for Black people walking down the streets of St. Louis. It's important to listen to these realities because that's what D&D does best. D&D allows communication between people with different backgrounds to find a common ground.

It turns out Omega, Shelly, and I have a lot in common through our history

---

1. Greg: Including many of the folks we've had on *Dragon Talk* and wrote about in this book, like Krystina Arielle, Tanya DePass, and B. Dave Walters.

with theater. I first learned about Omega as a performer and theater artist on Twitter through the fandom surrounding *Critical Role*, the voice actors who streamed their game and became a sensation. One day in 2017, he didn't have rehearsal for the show he was preparing at the time, and he was bored. "So I recorded [a cover of] the theme song to *Handbooker Helper*.[2] They liked it. They retweeted it. I became part of the community. Now we're all here," Omega said when we spoke in 2020. He downplayed how great the video he posted online really is—he took the harmonies in the seventeen-second theme and recorded four separate videos of him singing it in a way that seems totally standard on TikTok now but was way more of a novelty back then. Omega added some of his special vocal flair to the performance, of course. He is the Critical Bard after all.

The funny thing is that when he exploded onto the scene with that video, he had only been playing D&D for a little while. Omega admitted that he initially wasn't into D&D—but someone told him to think twice before he pooh-poohed it. "I looked at this *Dungeons & Dragons* game," he said, holding up a twenty-sided die like it was Yorick's skull. "And I said, 'Eww. What are you?'"

It wasn't until a theater director he was working with convinced him to attend a session with his tempest cleric Thotwar that the power of D&D was unlocked in Omega's brain.[3] He told us a wild story of how Thotwar eventually perished by using a magic item to its utmost extreme, and you can hear the excited theater person come out in Omega's telling, despite the fact that Thotwar was electrocuted while destroying a clockwork deva who was trying to end all life.[4] Sing aloud: "*Dungeons & Dragons*!"

"I did not expect to like this game as much as I do," he said. "You learn so much through this game, whether it's something about yourself or something you didn't know you could do."

---

2. Greg: *Handbooker Helper* was a short form web show produced by Geek & Sundry starring the *Critical Role* folks that gave info on playing D&D tuned for beginners. I always thought the title's pun was *chefs kiss* even if the food product it referenced wasn't always.

3. Greg: A tempest cleric is a priest of a stormy deity like Zeus or Poseidon, if you're up on your Greek myths. Omega named this character Thotwar just so he could say, "Be gone thot!" Look it up.

4. Greg: A deva is a D&D monster that is kind of like an angel. Muscly humanoid, big wings. They are usually good and will help the party, but they can be an adversary if the story is told right.

Omega found a significant creative outlet in this game that augmented the opportunities he didn't always have in the theater. "I've been acting professionally for ten or eleven years at this point," he said, and he didn't get a leading role until just a few years before this interview. He played Coalhouse in *Ragtime* and rocked it out of the park, winning all kinds of awards and, more importantly, additional roles after that performance. But Omega was quick to point out that his race had held him back in the theater world despite his abundant talents.

"You can get the fattest encyclopedia, almanac, whatever, you can throw that thing open and watch those pages fly and fly and fly, and while they're flying you can take a dart, you can go a mile away, and you can throw that dart and it will land in that book, and guess what? You can probably play that role, as a white person," Omega said, dramatically addressing his colleagues in the theater. "Me? I'm looking at the index going Coalhouse, Timon, Bernardo from *West Side Story*." There are so few musical theater roles written for people of color, and Omega has definitely been frustrated in not being able to work more in his chosen field.

That's one of the ways that playing D&D, singing about the game, and even applying makeup looks for his characters and sharing them with his fans online has enriched his life.

"This game has been for me personally one of the biggest creative outlets I've ever had. Ever," Omega said. "It's allowed me to just do things. And not about being fantastical like saying, 'I cast *fireball*!' It's not really about that, but there's something I take away from every single session I play, whether it's a longtime campaign or a one-shot. I leave that session feeling good. I leave that session feeling like I accomplished something."

"And if I can do that in-game, I can apply that to my real life," he continued. "I can do things and feel good about it in the end."

It's almost Zen the way he describes his relationship with D&D. During the interview, he repeated a phrase that my wife often says in times of hardship and good fortune: "Everything happens for a reason." I don't think he meant it in that "our fate is predetermined" kind of way but that it's important to realize every experience you have leads you to the next and there's no jumping the line. To wit: Omega wasn't ready to play D&D until he was ready to play D&D. "I picked up this game at the time I needed to pick it up," he said. If he had started playing earlier in his life, would the experience be as sweet? If he had skyrocketed to fame as an actor before he had to push through years of not being cast in leading roles, would he have had the right mix of talent and gravitas to bring to his performance? If he hadn't found D&D and an audience on Twitch, would he have had a creative outlet to perform when the pandemic hit and shut down live theater for more than a year? If Omega didn't become prominent in the D&D community by being the Critical Bard, would he have had the opportunity to speak truth to power when we needed it most?

That's what I hope people take away from D&D during times of political turmoil. I've said this a few times on the podcast, but I think one of the secrets of the success of *Dungeons & Dragons* right now was an indirect reaction to the Trump administration in the United States. So many of us felt terribly downtrodden after the election in 2016, and that feeling continued during the many horrors of the next four years, culminating in the pandemic and social unrest of summer 2020. So many of us felt powerless amid the endless news cycle of asshattery and were drowning in awful sound bites dipped in evil sauce. Feeling empowered to do something, *anything*, to fight the tyranny we were witnessing was important. D&D provided that artifice for a lot of us. Even if it was make-believe justice, it felt good.

When Omega Jones spoke his truth to his fellow D&D players on the "Black AF Roundtables," it felt natural. It felt like an extension of what so many of us were feeling. Enough was enough, and we were going to change what we could in our own space. We would be damned if we didn't speak truth to power in our own community!

So we did.

"I will never forget when I got the email saying 'Hey, we want you to do this Black AF panel at D&D Live.' I'm sorry, what?" he said. "That wouldn't have happened if those things didn't lead me to where it is now. And now I'm actively doing things with Wizards."

Amen to that.

As a coda, Omega certainly has an affinity with the power and magic of musical performance and that manifests perfectly in the bard class you can play in D&D. He has wonderful thoughts on how that class, and how elements of performance for all classes, can have a strong impact on storytelling at the table, and he discussed all those in a panel for D&D Celebration 2021 that brought many former *Dragon Talk* guests together. While everything we talked about is important, I'm pretty sure he would want to be remembered for his dynamic personality on stage and at the table.

"Whenever you need a reminder that 'Hey, this happened' or 'Hey this existed,' that's what I want to do as a bard," Omega said. "I want people to come to [see] me, and listen to me, and remember something. Whatever that something is, I don't necessarily know, but bards have that gift of unlocking that within people. Unlocking that forgotten memory, or that forgotten moment. If that makes someone happy, or that inspires someone, then why not keep doing it?"

RPG Road Tripping with
Hawke Robinson and John Welker

Confession: sometimes I hide chocolate from my son and eat it when he's not around. This means I'm usually consuming it in the bathroom. Eight-year-olds lack the sophistication to appreciate 100 Grand bars. I imagine this must have been what it felt like to play D&D in the 1980s. I hate bringing up the past as I know it's painful with the whole satanic panic and getting bullied for liking fantasy, and THAC0 deals.[1] D&D's early years were rife with stereotypes, divisiveness, and wild accusations. I mean, if these kids could really conjure demons, would there still be things like cafeteria pizza, SATs, and fluoride treatments? But I have some good news. Times have changed. D&D is actually good for you! There's data to back it up.

Today D&D is widely recognized as a bastion of creativity, collaboration, and imagination. Hawke Robinson and John Welker of RPG Research are putting actual science behind what longtime players already knew: D&D can make you a better, happier, smarter person. At least that's what I deduced from this interview.

Hawke and John have spent countless hours analyzing studies and conducting research proving that RPGs have a positive effect on one's well-being. This is not surprising, based on the D&D players I know. Hawke founded RPG Research, a nonprofit research and community services organization, to

---

1. Shelly: THAC0 is an acronym standing for "to hit armor class 0" and is possibly the most confusing rule in D&D's history. This was the number you needed to roll to hit that AC, which was considered good back then but is the functional equivalent of having an AC of 20 today.

help study the effects of all RPG formats (tabletop, live action, video games, computer-based, solo books, and modules) and their potential to improve lives. It's expanded into related areas, such as an interactive RPG museum, training, education, and public speaking, so if you want Hawke and John to come to your house and tell your parents you need more D&D books, they might be available. If you like research, you'll love their website. It houses the world's largest free and open research repository on roleplaying games. It's all volunteer run. These are two passionate gentlemen who want to bring awareness of this wonderful hobby to as many people as possible. One way to do that is road tripping around the country on a bus towing a trailer that serves as a wheelchair-accessible mobile gaming facility. They are literally bringing gaming to the masses.

RPG Research officially started in 1983, although one might argue it dated back to the 1970s, when Hawke was first introduced to D&D. A few years later, he wrote an eight-page essay on the myths and realities of roleplaying games and presented it to his whole elementary school. Take a minute to imagine yourself in 1983 reading a research paper to your peers arguing against all the negative stuff your parents and the media said about the hobby you love. This was just as the antigaming movement was kicking into gear, which made it an even bolder choice. While Hawke managed to sway the opinions of many of his schoolmates, the surrounding community was still dubious.

Then his school lost their drama teacher (to Broadway!) and all the theater kids got forced into study hall until a replacement was found. Never one to miss an opportunity, Hawke saw an opening and successfully pitched the headmaster on a roleplaying game class to take the place of drama. It was basically the same thing, right? Again, I ask you to imagine a world in which you gave up study hall for an actual class and were the one to teach it!

Fast forward to 2003. Hawke retired from his job as a computer scientist to focus on being a single parent. Like most parents, he wondered what he would do when his kids were grown and flown, but unlike me, his fantasy didn't involve a beach hut, naps, and a pinot grigio IV. Hawke had no intention of not working. He was a man with a plan, and the siren call to instill positive change in the lives of the most vulnerable communities could not be ignored. Hawke's always been a teacher in some capacity. He's proficient in lots of areas and loves guiding students in their quests for enlightenment. Because of his tech background, parents constantly asked him to help their kids with computer and typing classes. A lot of these kids were diagnosed with ADHD, so Hawke thought video games might be a clever way to help them focus and stay motivated. Kids loved playing video games. It hardly felt like school when you were doing something fun! It's probably obvious by now that Hawke was a bit of a savant and saw gaming as more than just a leisurely escape or pastime. The innate benefits were starting to bubble up even then. His intuition was spot on. The kids were thriving, having fun, and even learning. He created a rewards system granting them access to his lab so they could build their own computers and saw tremendous success with this approach. Then he found a way to combine his love of research, helping people, and music (he plays more than twenty instruments) by "falling into" recreation music therapy. Everything he was researching pointed to the same thing: recreation therapy is great, but more cooperative activities were needed. Hello! Hawke knew the answer.

This is the stuff that gets Greg and me really pumped. We know playing D&D is fun. But then there are organizations like RPG Research that see beyond the make-believe and magic. They knew there was a way to use RPGs to make a serious effect on the lives of the underserved. We're talking at-risk youth; kids and adults diagnosed with ADHD, autism, traumatic brain injuries, PTSD, depression, and anxiety; and people going through drug rehabilitation, just to name a few. Hawke set out to integrate roleplaying games into therapeutic settings and officially study the effects RPGs had on people. Time to send that whole satanic panic back to the Nine Hells.

Research study time. Do people who play RPGs have a higher rate of suicide than those who don't play RPGs? You might be thinking, "Jeez, Shelly! That got dark fast! Do your Bert impression from *Sesame Street* to cleanse the palate!" But bear with me. There was a time when people did make this correlation! In the 1980s, a grieving mother blamed D&D for her son's suicide, believing the curse placed on his character in game followed him in real life. Remember Pat Robinson and the *700 Club*? It was his mission to tell the world how D&D was destroying lives. Pat! Come on! D&D was saving lives!

Most of RPG Research studies were correlative, and here's where I get to sound like I know what I'm talking about. (In reality, I'm someone who had to listen to this part of the interview thirty-six times and Google a bunch of words to understand it.) Correlative research establishes a connection (but not necessarily causation) between two variables. Let's consider gamers and suicide rates. Research shows that gamers actually have a lower rate of suicide and depression compared with the general population. Huh. Who would have thought?

Another goal for RPG Research is to negate some dated stereotypes:

- Gamers are more likely to be depressed.
- Gamers are prone to violent crimes.
- Gamers are loners and outsiders.
- Gamers are a threat to themselves and others.

Studies showed that gamers had a higher sense of purpose in their lives, a lower criminality rate, and less violent personalities. Sorry Pat, but there's no proof D&D lures you away from religion and makes you side with the devil.

So gamers sound like pretty well-adjusted human beings. Why is that you ask? Again, I'm no expert, but here's what I deduced:

- Gamers are more likely to have friends! Most games, including D&D, require at least one other person. Games bring people together.
- Gamers have a stronger support system. We know how bonded gaming groups can be.
- Gamers are well versed in problem solving. Playing D&D requires quick thinking, analytical skills, and being able to use different strategies depending on the situation.
- Gamers are afforded a safe space for self-exploration. You can be anyone you want in D&D without judgment.
- Gamers are enormously empathetic. Interacting with flawed characters with different perspectives fosters broader thinking and social-emotional skills.
- Gamers have purpose. Thursdays aren't just the day before the day I drink a bunch of White Claws and fall asleep on the couch watching *Love Island UK*. It's my D&D day! Your weekly game night isn't just something to look forward to. Your party depends on you.

Hawke was also big into recreational therapy, the practice of using a recreational activity to achieve a therapeutic goal. Examples include playing *Uno* with a patient who suffered a brain injury and needed to relearn how to count or using Pick-a-Path books to stimulate the brain of someone recently woken from a coma. (The patient blinks or squeezes a hand as a way of choosing where the adventure takes them.) Hawke and his team put together a complete plan around RPG therapy for their patients, which included helping them find gaming groups to keep playing with after they leave therapy.

One of Hawke's mentors is a gentleman named John Dattilo who is a professor of health and human development at Penn State. He studies leisure, which sounds like an oxymoron but also makes me kind of want to go back to college and change my major. Part of Professor Dattilo's theory is that exploration is the foundation of learning. One day a baby discovers their hands, and suddenly the world materializes into a sensory paradise. One day a toddler masters mobility, and independence soon follows. The more elaborate and defined the details are, the more likely you are to remember it. I guess this is why my husband can remember everything that happened in a D&D game in summer 1987, but he never knew the name of our son's kindergarten teacher.

Exploration is the foundation of learning. Think about it. Exploration is also a foundation of roleplaying games: exploring new worlds, exploring new characters, exploring a collaborative story. Dattilo recognized Hawke's work and asked him to write a chapter about RPG therapy in the newest edition of his book, one of the most recognized resources in their field: *Facilitation Techniques in Therapeutic Recreation*. This meant recreational therapists all around the world and their patients would soon reap the benefits of Hawke's vision and RPG Research's work.

The next time someone asks why you play RPGs, tell them it's for the greater good. RPG players are making the world a better place, one die roll at a time. Believe science.

The Role Model of Tanya DePass

Before I met Tanya DePass for our first conversation on *Dragon Talk* in February 2017, I was just like every other bearded white dude: ignorant AF.

I didn't understand about how much adequate representation in our media helped people of color in our culture. I didn't fully grasp how characters with dark skin were hugely important to the Black community of D&D players, for better and for worse. I didn't even understand how decades of material published in D&D's past inadvertently (or extra-advertently, if that's a word) pushed people of color away from the game and how that mentality stretched into the social aspect around D&D tables at game stores and conventions. Which only pushed people further away.

Tanya talked about all these issues and more in our interview, and I can honestly say it was a turning point for me in my career and as a person. When gently confronted by the systemic racism she showed me in the game and how it was perceived, I decided to do everything I could to change it. Like most folks who suffer from procrastination, it took me a while to do anything substantial other than making a point to invite more people from marginalized groups to be guests on *Dragon Talk*.

A year after the interview, I reached out to Tanya again, and together we started making plans for what would become *Rivals of Waterdeep*, the first streaming D&D game funded by Wizards with the intention of only highlighting people of color in the cast. That included friends of Tanya's in the Chicago area, including Shareef Jackson and Cicero Holmes, former cohosts of a videogame podcast she was on for a couple years, and a Twitch streamer named Brandon Stennis, while I introduced them to two performers from the improv comedy scene, Carlos Luna and Surena Marie, who had done some audio-only D&D play for another podcast. We gathered the cast together, quickly signed contracts, and debuted *Rivals of Waterdeep* at the Stream of Many Eyes event a few months later. They played D&D together for the first time ever on stage in front of an audience in the studio and thousands of people online.

One of the most cherished moments of my career is from the welcome mixer for that event at a bar in L.A. when Tanya and the cast members of *Rivals* were in a circle talking to me and my wife. We were there, gin and tonics in hand, laughing about something one of them had said, but then it suddenly got really serious. They told me how much they appreciated me bringing them into the D&D community. Each of them said they had felt like outsiders for so long. Frankly, witnessing any effort by a major gaming company like Wizards to include people like them in D&D's premier marketing event meant more to them than anything else. We were all soon in tears.

I honestly didn't realize the impact D&D could have to work against the racism, oppression, and flat-out exclusion so many people of color experience in our culture. In the tabletop world, racism is sometimes expressed overtly, such as an overabundance of Nazi symbols in your opponents' wargaming heraldry, or, as Tanya mentions in the interview, when a white player really wants to play as a neutral evil slaver character when there's someone at the table whose ancestors experienced slavery. Those can be easy to spot, but small things can wear people down and push people away: the lack of any central characters with brown skin in the cover illustrations, the nervous glances from nerdy white folks when a person of color walks into a game store for the first time, the absence of Black Dungeon Masters at D&D events or conventions.

I couldn't do much to change racism everywhere, but I could make a few small decisions to make sure everyone felt welcome at our D&D events. I don't pretend like I'm special, I just listened to players like Tanya, just as any good Dungeon Master should. Every culture around the world tells stories and legends of heroes besting challenges. I tried to showcase talent from all those cultures because we all have a place at the table. The experience debuting *Rivals* and watching them grow and evolve over the years has galvanized me to do all I could to make sure D&D tables showed the full breadth of humanity going forward.

I chalk up all that to this conversation with Tanya. I had been following her on Twitter for a few years before our first interview on *Dragon Talk* as our video game predilections intersected a bunch. She was a fan of the *Dragon Age* CRPG series from BioWare,[1] and I had fondly watched her discuss *Dragon Age 2* on her Twitch playthroughs and on Twitter. We both loved that game, despite the internet being terrible about understanding why it's so good. During a small gaming convention called OrcaCon in the Seattle area in early 2017, she attended a talk by D&D lead rules designer Jeremy Crawford and live-tweeted her appreciation for things like the D&D fifth edition artwork portraying the default human fighter as a Black woman. At that time, I didn't realize she had any familiarity with D&D, so when I saw that thread, I asked her to join the podcast to talk about her fandom.

Shelly was unavailable for this interview, so I asked Bart Carroll to cohost with me since he had recently rejoined the D&D team and had grown up in the Chicago area.

Like me, Tanya grew up as a Roman Catholic, and we had similar problems trying to find a game we could play without catching our mothers' ire. As a teenager, she played RPG games to rebel, but it wasn't until the D&D 3.5 era (around 2005) that she found a group she could really gel with. Her DM created a homebrew world that Tanya explored for more than two and a half years. She fondly describes one of her early characters dying from a dragon's breath weapon. That character was an elf who never really got to delve into their amnesia, but upon that character's dramatic demise, she created a very different one: a hedonistic, lapsed paladin who was very honest about what she wanted and who she wanted it with.

"It was a great campaign," she said. "I traveled to the other side of the city to go play in this game." That's no small feat when all you have are the elevated trains to get across the many boroughs of Chicago. She did it for the love of the game and those she played with. "My friend North [the DM], I'm not sure if he will hear this, but he is a great DM and storyteller and crafter. It kept me engaged, and I just really loved it." Shout out to North!

Not everything about Tanya's experience playing D&D was positive. She was pretty upfront about players who, shall we say, endlessly pickpocketed their way through life. "Suddenly, this character who has no need of every

---

1. Greg: CRPG means computer roleplaying game, and the genre exists because early software designers emulated D&D mechanics in a digital game. *Dragon Age*, *Skyrim*, and *Final Fantasy* were all directly inspired by D&D, and you play that kind of game alone with your computer or console.

single thing we loot, suddenly needs to carry everything and I'm like, 'But you're a wizard and you can't even use that.'" For her, it is a combination of "folks not knowing how to resolve conflict and keep it away from the game setting" and general inexperience in life that comes with gaming with younger players. "Where are we going to sleep? You stole everyone's gold!" quipped Tanya.

She had good advice for that. "If there's interpersonal things that have nothing to do with the game, one thing you as a DM or you as a player can do if you want to make sure it doesn't creep into the game, is to try to talk about it well in advance of your next play session," she said. "Let's say you argue with someone two days before you are supposed to play. Even if it's sorta-kinda resolved, some people have a way of sneaking things 'in character.'" Oh, I recognize your joke about that blue dragon eating the last helping of pad thai in the fridge you were saving for lunch the next day wasn't really about D&D, was it? Let's maybe talk about that before we roll dice, hmm?

Tanya was quick to point out that conflict among characters can some-times lead to great storytelling at the table. "We as people are often told to avoid conflict," she said, acknowledging that not everyone wants to engage with real-world issues at the gaming table. "This is our fun time! We are going to sit around the table and throw dice and play pretend. Why would I want to bring active conflict into this setting? But for me, some of the greatest storylines I've had or interactions I've had is where canonically a character I'm playing has a disagreement or a story-driven reason to be in conflict with someone else. If I'm playing an elf or a dwarf, or whatever, and there's a way to weave that in without destroying the party." That's dramatic gold!

But—and this is a big "but"—it must be handled with extreme care, and Tanya was honest in saying that white people may not be the best equipped to, say, introduce a character dealing with the ramifications of slavery.

"You may say, 'I want to do a slaver class in my game' and the one person of color is looking at you like 'What? What did you say?'" she said pointedly. "Or you may want to give your character a backstory of having been a slave without thinking of the implications of that. In most cases, like 100 [percent], it is not appropriate because it is going to make everyone uncomfortable. This is going to sound bad, but I don't trust a non-person-of-color to handle that with sensitivity. . . . It's a big neon sign saying [to POC] you are not welcome."

Previously published lore around D&D peoples causes problems for a lot of Black people and other minorities when it is interpreted by years of white players dominating the conversation. Before this interview with Tanya, I had never heard the situation with the dark elves or drow in the game and surrounding novels explained so simply and, well, devastatingly.

"[Drow] are literally black," she said, describing how the drow elves had ebony skin in past editions of D&D. "And a lot of people use that as an excuse for racism. And blackface in cosplay."

Look no further than the season two episode of *Community* in which Señor Chang dons actual black makeup during their D&D session for an example.

"[Drow] are an evil race," she continued. "And the connotation that black is evil, dark [skin] is evil. . . . People have those associations and it's not an accident with 'dark' being associated with 'negative' and 'evil' and 'bad things.'"

Tanya acknowledged that one of the most iconic heroes in D&D is Drizzt Do'Urden, a dark elf who rejects his people's evil ways. That character can be a beacon for those who cherish seeing a character with dark skin like themselves in D&D lore. Even that concept is worth challenging because it reinforces the distinction between races that leads to the racism Tanya has experienced at the D&D table. Drizzt is great, but putting him forth as "model minority" who is "one of the good ones" is a difficult situation to praise unequivocally.

Tanya's experience is unfortunately all too common, and it was shaped by material and situations published decades ago. New rules have attempted to be more welcoming. For example, the fifth edition D&D game rules state that drow can have many different hues in their skin tone—ranging from ebony to blue or violet—and that their lineage doesn't shape their morality. That distinction was not noticed by every reader, who may have brought old assumptions into their games. Admittedly, even the fifth edition rules have not done an adequate job of removing all the biases that existed in the game since the 1970s, but the D&D team is committed to rectifying that with updates, errata, and new story elements. Continuing the example of the drow, it's now written that each drow society is influenced by different theologies,[2] and each drow is an individual capable of embracing or renouncing evil in their own choices. You know, just like all the people in our world.

That's something the designers of D&D are always striving to make clear to fans, and Tanya's willingness to work with Wizards of the Coast hinged on

2. Greg: To read about one such enclave, check out *Starlight Enclave* by R. A. Salvatore.

understanding that desire. "Jeremy did talk about that in his presentation [at OrcaCon 2017] and the origins of the drow and how they are trying to get away from that history of it and how people perceive the drow, and I was very happy to see that," she said.[3]

Combined with the interest drummed-up by Jeremy, and this interview on *Dragon Talk*, Tanya was excited to jump more fully into playing current D&D. "I want to do fifth edition, so obviously I need to get the books," she said, dropping the most transparent of hints to us running the brand. I sent her the *Player's Handbook* to get her started. That one little act may have woken the dragon.

Before I knew it, Tanya and I became friends collaborating on everything from streaming D&D games, raising money for charity, and bringing more people into the D&D community. She's been on *Dragon Talk* many times, even hopping on to help me by streaming a few of our introductions when Shelly wasn't available. I love seeing her at gaming conventions like PAX or Geek Girl Con, and she's always a text message away if I need someone to absorb my venting or answer tough questions. I'm proud of what she's done producing *Rivals of Waterdeep*, keeping it going by adding new cast members for more than ten seasons, four years, and 100 episodes. She's also working with B. Dave Walters on the *Black Dice Society* streaming game and developing her own roleplaying games, all while being a prominent voice for people of color in the D&D community. I get the feeling she's just getting warmed up, kind of like getting to the later stages of her life as a red dragon, about to add about ten more d6s to her breath weapon.

All of that can be traced back to when Tanya, Bart, and I talked openly about her experiences on *Dragon Talk*. This game forges connections that can help heal so much. What are you waiting for? It's time to play D&D.

3. Greg: Jeremy Crawford is the lead rules developer for D&D fifth edition, and his talk at OrcaCon is what brought Tanya and me together.

D&D Is in Session with Steve Hobbs

t's not every day a state senator comes to your office and geeks out about your day job. But if it's Washington state senator Steve Hobbs and your day job is brand manager for *Dungeons & Dragons*, it would be an everyday occurrence.[1]

Serving as a member of the Washington State Senate since 2006 and as a lieutenant colonel in the Washington Army National Guard at the time of our interview, Senator Hobbs was an uber geek who split his time between sessions in Olympia, Washington, and sessions around his gaming table. He grew up with a love of gaming after discovering D&D in the 1970s. Like most kids when they start playing, he didn't always have a grasp of the rules, but filling in holes and making up his own guidelines was part of the fun. He kept up with it for nearly two decades until his military obligations left him with little time to play. Our interview wasn't even his first visit to Wizards of the Coast. He stopped by once with a more formal agenda and managed to squeeze in a quick game with Chris Perkins. It was short and sweet, and fifth edition reignited his love of D&D. It was the perfect escape for a busy, nerdy politician. He's found ways to couple his professional and fantasy lives, proposing laws benefiting the games industry in Washington state.

I got a little nervous before Senator Hobbs showed up because he was, you know, an elected official. Were there rules about talking to a state senator? Are we banned from asking specific questions? Do we curtsy? Can he get us out of speeding tickets? Why wasn't there a *Schoolhouse Rocks* ditty about

1. In November 2021, Senator Hobbs became Secretary Hobbs after being appointed Washington's sixteenth Secretary of State.

hosting senators on your podcast? We probably should have raised the American flag or something.

I shouldn't have been worried considering how hard Senator Hobbs was lobbying to be our guest. His first email asked if he could come on the show to promote OrcaCon, a budding tabletop game convention in the Seattle suburbs he was heavily involved in. And he hosted his own podcast called *Geeks of Cascadia*, a self-described "nerdy little tabletop games podcast" featuring interviews with game developers, publishers, artists, and more. The subject line of his email was "10th Level Politician Senator Steve Hobbs makes Persuasion check with his Blue samurai disguise," and it was dripping with geekiness and shameless self-promotion. Like it was so nerdy, I'm not even sure Greg got all the references.

He also wrote, "After all, ask yourself, have you two interviewed a politician before? The answer is NO because I have listened to nearly EVERY *Dragon Talk* episode."

Oh, he was also a *Dragon Talk* fan? Now we were truly freaked out! We failed to respond right away because we thought it might have been a joke. A senator? Who wants to be interviewed on *Dragon Talk*? Even after hearing our poop jokes and Muppet impressions? Nah. Definitely a phishing scam. But then we got a follow-up email saying even if we couldn't fit him in, he'd still be a big fan of the show and ended by saying we were awesome!

I made Greg write him back because this felt like a job for the senior communications manager. Can anything you say to a state senator in a poorly worded, misspelled email be used against you? Could that bogus open container violation from college that was expunged from my record be . . . re-punged?

As much as I appreciated the flattery and salesmanship, he had us at *state senator*, I like to maintain an aspirational air. It's not just compliments that will get you a booking. We also like swag.

As soon as Senator Hobbs sat down he said again on air he was a huge fan of *Dragon Talk*. This was still a bit incredible, so I asked him if he really knew where he was right now. Maybe his assistant just told him the address and whom to ask for. Maybe there was another podcast with a similar name? *Drag and Talk*? (Now *that* sounds cool!) Nope, he was a real fan of the show. He referenced several of our past guests. He knew about the untimely and no-fair fall of my beloved country that one time I played Diplomacy. He related to our theater kid backgrounds because he happened to be one too. As cool as being in the home of his favorite pastime was for him, Greg and I were nerding out at the fact we were sitting down with the first ever elected official to be a guest on *Dragon Talk*. First and only, as it turns out. At least until he gets more of his colleagues playing.

The interview was on Monday, which coincidentally was his weekly game night. He was playing a wizard in a *Waterdeep: Dragon Heist* campaign. Typically he favored fighters because there was less thinking and more doing, and I guess when you spend your days thinking and doing, it's kind of refreshing to just mindlessly burst through a wooden door. He never played a character with a political background for obvious reasons.

Surprisingly there were not a lot of nerds in state assemblies. Allegedly. I'm guessing in an industry where image is everything, anything even remotely polarizing was shoved deep in the basement along with your old goldenrod character sheets and blue d20s with white crayon colored numbers. I'm certain Bart and I were not cast on HGTV's *House Hunters* because of D&D! After making it through several rounds of casting and assurances from the producer that the HGTV executives just *loved* us, some muckety muck must have rewatched our audition tape and heard us say we needed lots of storage space for Bart's G.I. Joe dolls, my twenty-three artificial Christmas trees, and our weekly *Dungeons & Dragons* game nights. But that's a story for another time.

Senator Hobbs was not concerned about image. Or if he was, he clearly didn't think being a gamer was bad for his persona. He wore his geekiness like it was Armor of Invulnerability. He even had a "nerd corner" in his office where he had his D&D books, giant d20, comic books, and *Star Blazers* wares on display. A nerd corner is not common on the hill, but it is a great conversation starter. If someone recognizes the d20, they get to place a speed bump on the street of their choice in their county.

The "nerd corner" isn't the only way he's rolling for initiatives. Senator Hobbs is passionate about fostering growth in our local gaming industry and shining a light on its importance to the state economy. There's almost as many game companies in the Seattle area as there are drive-up coffee shops and Subarus. Pokémon, Green Ronin, Valve, Paizo, Bungie, and Microsoft, to name a few. Game companies don't just employ thousands of people, they help support the surrounding communities. When you get a hotbed of game publishers in one region, you attract a lot of artists, writers, designers, and passionate gamers. Then come the hobby game shops and conventions, which pump a steady stream of revenue into the hospitality industry. Hobbs's initiatives aren't just about manufacturing, tax credits, and scoring cool branded coffee mugs from his favorite publishers. He had this wild idea about helping freelancers acquire affordable health care and pensions. People who spend their days pretending to be elves and wizards and telling stories together are generally very nice, cool people, and who wouldn't want more of them in their community?

You may think Washington's biggest export was aerospace parts and salmon, but not if Senator Hobbs has his way.

"We're exporting *fun*," he claimed, which spawned the first of my lobbying attempts. Sure, the Evergreen State has a nice ring to it, but I proposed a new state motto: Where the Magic Happens. I got a polite, "Ohhh," from Senator Hobbs. But my second, more straightforward idea got a much better reception: put a giant Tiamat statue at Seattle-Tacoma International Airport with a plaque that reads, "Welcome to Seattle: Home of *Dungeons & Dragons*."

Senator Hobbs felt like he could validate this idea because Tiamat was female, representative of the diverse D&D community, and a strong leader. A true emblem of empowerment!

"She's also evil," said Greg, the buzzkill.

"But she's lawful evil," Senator Hobbs noted, once again waving that nerd flag. "She obeys the law, but it's *her* law."

Although there aren't many out and proud roleplayers in the state senate, there really should be. Greg offered to run a game for our state's politicos if Senator Hobbs could get a group together. D&D can bring the parties together to show how people with different affiliations can work together for a common goal. Plus we share the same lingo (sessions, initiatives, parties—the puns just write themselves here). Just imagine our little game being what unifies this country. Just please don't ask them to play Diplomacy.

shelly

Dungeons & Dragons 101
with Ethan Schoonover

You've heard the stories, heeded the warnings, stayed awake at night, and were haunted by the plights of hallowed heroes who ended up on the wrong side of the field. Was it something you said? Something you wore? Something you dared pull from your rucksack to sate your appetite during a short rest? You knew your day would come. This rite of passage spared no one. A place where no one was welcome, where outsiders were sniffed out like the fang-filled mouth of an otyugh and exploited like a Real Housewife's dirty secret. Packs of she-wolves lay in wait, noses pressed to the night sky waiting for the faintest hint of insecurity, doubt, and Love's Baby Soft. Regardless of which god you bowed down to, which pact you vowed to keep, you too would have to face the beast staring you down from the fiery pits of hell.

Welcome to middle school.

Or at least, that's how I remember it. Remember when schools had to be remote because of the COVID-19 quarantine and everyone felt bad for elementary school kids who were desperate for a foursquare game and high schoolers missing out on major milestones and formative memories? No one felt bad for the middle schoolers. Those kids had been given a gift from Bahamut himself.

Middle school was not my favorite era, and we didn't even have social media to contend with. I wanted to be like everyone, but also different. I wanted cool friends, but the cool kids were stuck up and boring. I wanted to go on a date, but the thought of talking to a boy forced me to stuff my head in my locker and pant into the lunch bag my mom packed with Ring Dings and Cool Ranch Doritos. (I guess not all of middle school was bad.)

Were my jeans too tight or my sweaters too baggy? Would I be eating lunch with the cool South Side kids or would Tara Clark tell everyone she wanted to kick my ass after school today?[1] Would I be labeled a loser if I was too smart in language arts? Was it cool to fail a math test?

I remember Ryan Percy pointing out the giant zit that spent so much time on the side of my nose in eighth grade that my brother named it Zeek Pussfield, and Sarah Sweeny calling me "monkey girl" because my arms were hairy. Come on, Sarah. That's not even clever. Even "gorilla girl" has more pizzazz. Ever hear of alliteration? Do better.

Today I'm a certified grown-ass woman and still incredibly awkward around tween and teen girls. A few years ago, my friend Kristina had a party for her twelve-year-old daughter, who is pretty much the greatest kid in the world. I give her pizza and homemade brownies and she gives me the scoop on who likes who, who posts questionable content on TikTok, and why sipping from the wrong water bottle will completely tank any chance you have of going to prom. Kristina rented a space at her neighborhood community center, and I volunteered to help, thinking it would be fun to hang with my bestie and pretend we were annoyed by Taylor Swift while singing every word to every song. One minute I was happily filling plastic bowls with Pirate's Booty and laying out star-shaped eyeglasses and tiaras for the photo booth, and two seconds after the first girl rolled in I was clammy, sheepish, and hiding in the kitchen sneaking swigs of Clementine vodka from a certified uncool water bottle. Yep. Just like middle school. I had to keep reminding myself "I am the adult!" Surely these girls could see what a cool, chill mom-lady I was with my chipped manicure, stretched-to-capacity skinny jeans, and ankle booties. Oh God, was I trying too hard? Was I a decade too late for a wedge heel? The awfulness of my cuticles was enhanced by the Pirate Booty cheese dust clinging to my fingertips. I was a monster!

You can take the girl out of middle school, but you can't take the middle school out of the girl. If you attend Lake Washington Girls Middle School, that might not be a bad thing. Get this—there is a world in which middle school doesn't suck. For girls. And it's because of *Dungeons & Dragons*.

You're probably asking yourself what alternate reality we are living in where these three things go together, but trust me—they do. I can't speak for

---

1. Shelly: Obviously these names are made up. I may still be a little afraid of the real "Tara Clark."

all middle school girls (clearly), but it's definitely the hotness (OMG who says "hotness"?) at Seattle's North Beacon Hill neighborhood with the mission of empowering girls to be strong in mind, body, and voice. But how? Allow me to introduce you to Ethan "Mr. E" Schoonover.

Ethan is a local legend. A father, a tech professional, and a practicing sorcerer, he spent some time dabbling in the marketing and software space (as one does in the Pacific Northwest). After logging some volunteer hours at the school, he marveled at how fulfilled and invigorated he felt and thought, "Hey, maybe this could be a job."

"You mean teaching?" Greg and I asked. "Umm, yep, that's a job."

Shortly after, Ethan was hired to teach programming.

Now Ethan is a jeans and blazer kind of guy. Probably has a few corduroy jackets with elbow patches for those fancy nights on the town.[2] Pretty standard garb for a literate, technically gifted, PNW dad. But to a twelve-year-old student who rolled high on her Insight check, he might as well have been draped in mage armor and a pointy hat.

"Mr. E?" she began, looking around to ensure no one could overhear. "Have you seen *Stranger Things*?"

"Uh, yeah," he answered. "I've seen it."

What was going on here? He thought. Was she about to open a briefcase and try to shill some knock-off Duffer brothers merch?

"Have you, uh, seen the D&D stuff in it?" she asked.

"Yep, I did."

"So, do you . . . know how to play D&D?"

Turns out he did. Some people just give off the vibes.

Ethan grew up right in D&D's backyard in Wisconsin. He started dabbling in the D&D arts in the 1970s after his "hippie parents" gifted him the Red Box and he continued to adventure well into the 1980s. When approached by this perceptive young woman, he was just starting his return to roleplaying games.

Mr. E admitted that not only did he know how to play, he was thinking of starting a D&D club. Roll for initiative! It was literally game on for this girl, or rather, daily bombardment asking when this club was happening.

"When are we playing D&D?" she demanded on the regular.

Greg and I were impressed. This girl had no experience playing D&D, but

2. Greg: Hey, wait a minute! That's my signature look!

saw it portrayed on a show where a child about her age was abducted and taken to an alternate dimension by a mysterious creature and his friends and a telepathic girl needed to rescue him from a freaky, giant, tentacled monster and evil government scientists and thought, "Yes! I want in on that action!" I guess that does sound kind of cool. But D&D was around when I was in middle school and I had no desire to take down a Demogorgon in the science lab. Or even know where the science lab was.

Everyone who has ever gone to a school knows Friday afternoon is the worst time for a club to meet. Kids and teachers are just done. Why stick around school longer than you needed to?

"So that's exactly when the D&D club met," Ethan said, almost hoping the girls would be too tired and burned out to show up.

But they showed up. At first, the club topped off at four, which was more than fine for Ethan, who had never DMed for more than three and never for tween girls. (I'll take Demogorgon in the science lab, thanks.) But then a fifth student showed up and what choice did he have but to let her play? A little while later, the father of another student got wind of what was going on and called Ethan.

Oh no! Ethan was in *trouble*! Who's this guy teaching these nice girls how to wield two-handed weapons and banish demons back to hell? I went straight into Lifetime Television for Women territory. I could see the preview now: This Friday, don't miss, *A Father's Initiative* starring Tony Danza and Mario Lopez. Oh man, that's pretty good. How do I write a treatment?

"Did he want to fight you?" I asked.

"No, he asked if I could get his daughter in the club," Ethan explained.

Cool story, but mine is better.

They say location is everything, and it's not only true for 600-square-foot fixer-uppers with a water view. The dean of teaching was kind enough to offer space in her office for the fledgling D&D club. At first she didn't pay much attention except for a quick glance upward when girls became more exuberant. But week after week, hearing the enthusiasm and creativity coming from this group, the dean could tell something special was happening. She asked Ethan if he would be interested in teaching a D&D class. No, not like a "here's how to make a ranger" tutorial. Like a *Dungeons & Dragons* class with a D&D–based curriculum. The girls would learn how to play, and like one of those weird toddler food pouches, all the less appetizing stuff was masked by the sweet, sugary, magical goodness. Under Ethan's guidance, the girls learned math principles and creative writing. Local artists, D&D streamers, and authors like Jen Vaughn, Kate Welch, and Kat Kruger visited the class to talk about their passion for the game. Although it was capped at only eight students, the class quickly grew in popularity, leading to the next evolution: D&D summer camp.

Ethan can't say no to things, which is why he's such a great dad and Dungeon Master. Of course he said yes to leading a D&D–themed summer camp. Amazing, right? After a summer of adventure, questing, and improv, camp culminated with archery lessons, because no matter what class we play, there's a little ranger in all of us.

The D&D club, class, and camp attracted more than a third of the entire school and could have drawn more if he had additional Dungeon Masters. There was no way Mr. E could DM for all thirty girls who signed up, and recruiting and training other adults who were already juggling day jobs and family life proved to be an exercise in futility. There was only one viable option: the students must surpass the master. The Dungeon Master, that is.

"That's a huge accomplishment," Ethan explained. "At that age, to manage your peers?"

Not to mention public speaking, expertise, improv, and leadership. You know, life skills. But who would take up the mantle?

Ethan went back to the OGs—the self-titled group of five "original gamers." Two immediately volunteered, and when he asked them to recommend a third, they chose someone he didn't expect. Ethan thought she was a little on the quiet side and maybe DMing would put her off, but her peers saw something in her.

While shy and subdued in real life, this girl came alive at the table, creating colorful characters and adding a unique perspective to every challenge, exactly the traits that make for a great storyteller. Here at this amazing school, the girls sniffed out something different and celebrated it.

Dungeon Masters are obviously key to playing D&D, but it's a lot of work. These girls didn't see it that way. Turns out Dungeon Mastering was straight fire. (If you're not as up on the lingo as I am, that means, it was "pretty dang cool.") To them it was an honor to be selected. It didn't hurt that Ethan orchestrated a ceremony, handing each newly minted DM an oversized d20. The Dungeon Master training program grew to where they had ten young women in regular rotation. They naturally discovered co–Dungeon Mastering where they would jointly lead the group, playing on each other's strengths, picking up where the other left off, and trading responsibilities. There was a noticeable change in the D&D–playing girls. They were becoming more outgoing, more confident, and more creative. Soon they were writing and running their own adventures. Ethan's D&D efforts were revered by parents and teachers alike, as part of a much different world than the one a lot of kids in the 1980s grew up in. One student told Mr. E that her parents noticed the change in her. Before she had a "school self" and a "home self" and never the twain could meet. But D&D let her be both, and both were pretty special.

I couldn't help but wonder if Ethan would have seen something special in middle school Shelly, the attention-seeking weirdo who acted out soap opera scenes with her stuffed animals and spent all summer in the library plowing through Jackie Collins's and Danielle Steel's extensive literary catalog. Or . . . not. But I'd still love to audit the Dungeon Master training program.

All good things must come to an end, or in this case, graduate. Unlike my middle school, the Lake Washington Girls Middle School was a place one might want to cling to. Sure, it's sad to see the OGs and the girls who followed their pioneering footsteps graduate out of the program, but they level up and take their experience points with them.

"One of the girls who graduated is now running the D&D club in high school," Ethan told us.

Not just high school—a coed high school. While the soon-to-be graduate was pondering the possibility of boys joining the club, one of the younger girls offered advice: "It's okay if a boy wants to play. Try to accept them too."

D&D was *their* thing. A girl's game. One in which they felt empowered, protected, celebrated, and victorious. There is no doubt these girls will grow up to become the kind of women Beyoncé sings about.

I had so many questions for Ethan, but he had a family and a job and one of the coveted two-hour visitor parking spots in front of our office, so we had to let him go. But one last inquiry: "Was it hard for the girls to hurt animals?"

"Funny you should ask," Ethan answered. "In one game the girls were tasked with saving a girl who was kidnapped by kobolds."[3]

Ethan realized midway through combat he was essentially encouraging them to murder kobolds, which didn't feel right. It was a great time for a lesson in morals and ethics, so he taught them about alignment.

---

3. Shelly: Kobolds are reptilian, dragon-worshiping humanoid creatures commonly found in dungeons.

"They managed to save the girl and decided they didn't need to kill the kobolds after all."

How wonderful, I thought! There are many ways to solve a problem and violence doesn't have to be one of them. A great lesson for all middle school kids. (I'm looking at you, Tara Clark.)

"But they left the kobolds tied up," Ethan continued, "and a pack of wolves came by and ate them."

Ah, right. Now *that* sounds like middle school.

Deborah Ann Woll Pushes Story

Navigating small failures is something D&D teaches you very well. When everything piles up and it feels like I've rolled a failure in my life, I often think of something Deborah Ann Woll said during our first interview on *Dragon Talk*. There was an event she described with Joe Manganiello's character, and Matt Mercer as DM,[1] that feels important to me. "There's a moment . . . that involves my character failing an ability-saving throw," Deb said, not wanting to give anything away. "The thing that Matt and I talked about a lot before this session is that sometimes failures are even better than successes. They push story. Instead of going, 'Ah dammit, I didn't do it!' [you should] go 'Oh great, now I get to dive wholeheartedly into living what this experience is for this character.'"

Deborah dove wholeheartedly into her performance in *True Blood* on HBO. The tragic first appearance of her character Jessica as a young girl forced to be transformed into a vampire is terrifyingly compelling. That character wasn't even supposed to be a big part of the series, but Deb stuck with it. Her growth in later seasons as a woman struggling to control her abilities and her relationships with human men with varying success was a well-crafted coming-of-age metaphor. When Nathan Stewart and I would talk about performers we wanted to recruit to play D&D at events, Deb was someone we always thought was a total long shot—a DC 25 level challenge that would take a very high Persuasion check to succeed. But think of what Matt Mercer taught Deb in that quote above: failures are stronger than successes. You have to embrace what happened and move your story forward. Just like your character does every time they roll a natural 1 and fumble that shit.

1. Greg: Mercer is the DM from *Critical Role* and a helluva great person.

After a few years of failing to convince Deborah to roll dice with us, Nathan finally hit the mark in 2017 with the filming of a promotional series called *Force Grey: Lost City of Omu*, which we premiered on the Nerdist channel, back when that was a thing.

The first time I got to meet her was when we spoke with her for *Dragon Talk* in July 2017 promoting that series. I was struck by her authentic fondness for D&D. She got it. She dug it. She was very much *into* D&D in a way that felt refreshing.

I've gotten to know Deb more over the years by asking her to Dungeon Master for D&D Live and to get involved with stuff on the creative side of the game. Her game *The Witch of Briarcleft* at the Stream of Many Eyes in 2018 is still my wife's go-to example for explaining to people the power of storytelling through roleplaying games to nonfans, as the fairy-tale story Deb brought to life was full of funny moments, confounding puzzles, and evil twists. I've watched her confidence at the table grow, and I've been happy to be a small part of encouraging that growth. I wouldn't say we're best buds or anything, but I think I can say we are work friends, excited to see each other to catch up once in a while. When the work brings us together again, I'm grateful for that connection because I always feel like I learn something about myself.

When Shelly and I first interviewed Deb, I was surprised to hear that she had only recently come to playing D&D. "It's only been like five years, I think, since I've been into it," she said. "I've always been really curious about it, but I wasn't even cool enough to hang with the D&D folk in my school. So I couldn't get into it then, but I was always interested. It turns out one of my managers at the time had been playing for a long time and DMing for a number of years. So I told him about it and he's like, 'We'll get a group together!'"

She played with that group for a while and started telling her own stories as DM a couple of years after that. She's very good at on-boarding new players to D&D. She developed an adventure involving the Raven Queen that she'd run for anyone interested in learning about the game. "Any friend who knows that I play D&D and is like, 'What is it? I don't know what D&D is? I've always heard these rumors.' I've whittled it down to this great simple one-off module so I can just be like, 'Hey, come over for four hours. Play. See if you like it. See what it is.' So yeah, it's turned out to be this useful tool."

The interactivity that's possible around the D&D table is greater than even the connection to the audience that live theater is sometimes known for. "It almost doesn't even compare with D&D," Deb said. "There was a moment the other day where I had six people sitting around the table and [in-game] they had already rolled three or four dice rolls to attempt to wake this girl up who was in this enchanted sleep. They were going to give up, but they convinced [a player] to try one more time. It was just enough, and I had these six faces staring at me. And I just said, 'Her eyes flutter . . .' and they all jumped up and screamed! Not even in live theater do you get that kind of excitement and reaction from people."

It's clear that D&D is really important to Deb. For a long time, she was reluctant to do anything publicly with the game since it was the source of so much consistent joy. I understood when she told us acting isn't always full of said joy. "I love acting. I've done it my whole life. It brings me a crazy amount of joy, but there's so much stress and anxiety that goes with it that it is rarely ever just purely joyful," she admitted.

In 2017, Deb was about to go to the premiere of *The Defenders*—the Marvel miniseries that combined four of their series together into four action-packed episodes. Her performance as Karen Page in the *Daredevil* and *Punisher* series was widely acclaimed, but not all of those series were a success, and their future in the Marvel cinematic universe even now is not confirmed. For all its supposed glamour, acting really is just hustling to book as many freelance gigs as you can. The stress and anxiety of not knowing when your next job is going to come can really pull you down, and Deb wanted her time at the table to fly free from those feelings, like a fairy fluttering on the breeze.

"The wonderful thing about D&D is that pretty much every time I play it, it is nothing but joyful," she said. "There's just nothing else in my life that gives me that."

She was concentrating on avoiding the failure state, but what if the work brought joy too? What if the creative work was more closely linked to the joyful work of DMing for friends?

Her appearance on *Force Grey* as Jamilah, a badass barbarian from Chult, was her first foray into playing D&D for an audience. She played alongside *True Blood* costar Joe Manganiello, Brian Posehn, Utkarsh Ambudkar, and Dylan Sprouse, with Matthew Mercer as DM. Deb's character was a strong combatant and cocksure, which she used as a way to combat her own reluctance.

"I'm not always very confident," she said. "I wanted Jamilah to be super confident because I was so nervous about coming in and doing *Force Grey*. So I thought I'll play a really super confident character and that will mask how nervous I am."

Shelly and I were impressed. "Does that work?" I said.

Apparently, it did, since she knocked that role out of the park for seventeen episodes, which were edited down from two days of playing D&D for eight hours each. The funny thing was that it was the culmination of playing something like twenty-seven hours of D&D over a four-day span for Deb, because she had spent the two previous days playing with friends. That's about 359 dice rolls, 5,890 hit points of damage, and 14,000 Cheetos consumed. She couldn't get enough!

Force Grey cracked the protective shell she had separating the game from her acting career, and she fully embraced her skills as a storyteller and a Dungeon Master. Like how her character embraced being a vampire on *True Blood*, she latched on to the idea of D&D bringing her professional joy. Deb created her own fantasy show called *Relics & Rarities* for the Geek & Sundry network, when that was a thing. That series featured a custom-made set of a curiosity shop and a strong regular cast who meet a special guest character played by the likes of Janina Gavankar, Sam Richardson, Matthew Lillard, Charlie Cox, and Kevin Smith for a new mystery each week. The show was a brilliant execution blending imagination and TV production, including lighting and props, to create something special, as well as bringing new people into the game. It was really magical.

The next time she came on *Dragon Talk* was to promote her running a *Relics & Rarities* game at D&D Live 2019, almost two years after our first conversation. Deb was a bit more open about how that initial reluctance to publicly present herself as the D&D–playing woman she was had completely evaporated. She had embraced it fully, running a campaign for the former manager who taught her how to play D&D, while producing original content using the game as a framework.

But you could tell Deb wanted to focus on her acting career again. "I'm taking a bit of a break from D&D at the moment," she said. "I'm in a transitionary period in my work-work so I'm focusing a little there and trying to see if I can continue to do my job." Then 2020 happened and everyone in the entertainment industry had to pump the brakes as things shifted and changed for the global pandemic. Life is like a d20. You are just as likely to roll a 1 as you are to get a critical hit.

That's how it works sometimes. My wife was an actress but never saw the success she thought she would. I wanted to be a playwright or even a standup comedian, but opportunities for those types of jobs can feel out of your control. The hustle sucks. I'm funny, dammit. Doesn't anyone want to give me food for it? People who dream to create things can cut themselves down quick when projects don't work out. You have to find your own journey and your own successes, even if you don't know exactly what you are going to find at the end of your quest called life.

Just like Matt Mercer told Deb back when they were filming *Force Grey*, "Sometimes failures are even better than successes. They push story. Instead of going, 'Ah dammit, I didn't do it!' [you should] go 'Oh great, now I get to dive wholeheartedly into living what this experience is for this character.'"

That's pretty good advice for all of us. Thanks, Deb.

greg

Kyle Balda Real-Time Directs D&D

You may not know the name Kyle Balda, but you know the animation projects he's worked on throughout his career. He was director and creative driver for *Minions*, *Despicable Me* 3, and *The Lorax*, and he came up in the animation business working on Pixar films like *A Bug's Life*, *Toy Story* 2, and *Monsters, Inc.* He even worked as an animator on the classic LucasArts game *Day of the Tentacle*. While his career was blossoming for a decade in Paris, where Illumination had an animation studio, he had stopped playing D&D. But like many of our guests on *Dragon Talk*, he was getting back into it with a vengeance thanks to the fifth edition. Kyle's son had a big role to play there, and the director was fascinated by what the game could teach him about storytelling techniques. Or maybe, as we found out through the course of this hard-hitting interview, that early experience with D&D had already taught him all he knew.

Kyle's story begins in Malta. His mother was a native of the small island off the coast of Sicily in the Mediterranean Sea. Listening to Kyle talk about the nation, it's no wonder to me how much fantasy and myth played into his life's story. He didn't grow up there, but its DNA may have led to his desire to draw fantastic locations and characters. "Valletta, which is the capital of Malta, is a fortified city right on the water, there's these amazing walls jutting out of the water," he said. "And then you have really old Neolithic—is that the word?—kinda like Stonehenge type of druid formations all over the island."

A fascination with myth and a lack of interest in other scholarly matters led Kyle to art and fantasy. "When I was in a library for whatever reason I had to be in a library, because I wasn't very academic as a youngster, I always used to love to draw," he said. "I'd go to the mythology section and pull out Greek mythology books and just look at the pictures." That stuff sparked something inside him that combined with his drive to create. "I was really into knights and chivalry, and for Halloween I would make suits of armor out of duct tape and cardboard."

The ingenuity to make something awesome paid off early with more inspiration fuel. "There was a cinema near my house, and during the summer I would go there and ask if I could draw advertisements for popcorn and Coca-Cola and stuff so I could get into the movie theater for free," he said. "I would go and sit and watch movies nonstop and that's when I saw Ralph Bakshi's *Lord of the Rings* and *Clash of the Titans* and all these movies that echoed back the stuff I loved."

Around the same time, young Kyle would head to the mall to play *Dragon's Lair* at the arcade or peruse the D&D books at the local hobby shop. "I had no idea what they were, but the images on the covers of the books really spoke to me," Kyle said. He started collecting all the accoutrements around D&D, like the books and the dice, but he didn't know how to put it all together to form a game. Enter his cousin Michael. He had been playing the game for a while since he was a couple years older than Kyle, and they got to talking. Before Kyle knew it, Michael asked him if he wanted to play D&D right then.

"He had a paladin, which instantly I loved, because of that old David Sutherland image 'A Paladin in Hell' in the old player's handbook just really caught my imagination, so I was like 'Yes, I wanna play a paladin,'" he said. "He had this paladin named Scorch, and he said, 'Okay you can play Scorch and I'll DM you.' We just did this theater of imagination thing."

I love how, right there in the middle of a big Maltese family get-together, a random D&D game broke out. It was eye-opening for Kyle that just asking a few questions helped his cousin weave a compelling story, the details of which still stuck in his mind decades later. "I remember I had to fight these giant frogs at some point." He was disappointed when his cousin's parents had to leave the party early that night, but Kyle had gotten a taste for D&D, and he was hooked.

He soon found friends at school who were excited to play with him, and he went through many of the touchstones many D&D fans had growing up in the 1980s, like playing the *Queen of the Demonweb Pits* and *Ravenloft* modules but with perhaps more of an emo/art school bent. "I got super hooked at drawing elves, and drawing Lolth," Kyle said with a laugh. "She's still my favorite D&D

villain."[1] He and his friends would switch around the roles of acting as a DM and run fantastic stories for each other. One of them, Darren Davis, was an inspiration to combine art with storytelling through the medium of comic books.

Kyle took that portion of his fandom and forged a career out of it. On the advice of family friend Dan Jupe, who was a Disney animator then working on *The Little Mermaid*, he refined his drawings to show more motion and eventually took courses at CalArts in L.A. "'You're drawing like an illustrator. Animators draw life, rather than light,'" he said Jupe told him. He took that advice all the way to internships at little outfits you may have heard of, like LucasArts Games and a computer animation studio called PDI, which was later subsumed into Dreamworks after making films like *Shrek* and *Madagascar*.

Then *Jurassic Park* came out in 1993. Kyle didn't work on that film, but he did say how the demand for computer animators in Hollywood skyrocketed. "*Jurassic Park* came out that summer and things just exploded," he said. "There were tons and tons of movies with 3D animated visual effects . . . I stopped going to school because I got a job at ILM." That's the visual effects studio created by George Lucas for the *Star Wars* films, and it was still a pioneer in the special effects world.

Press fast forward on the animated film of Balda's life and you'll zoom past amazing moments like working at Pixar in the 1990s and 2000s and moving to Paris full-time to work for Illumination and creating the iconic characters of Minions. He married, had children, and moved back to the United States after finishing the last film, *Minions: The Rise of Gru*. I picked up my finger from the fast forward button to see Kyle walking on the beach in Santa Monica with his son and his son's girlfriend. The bright Cali sun shone down on them as the sea spray, fierce-burning incense, and weight-lifting grease fills the air.

"[We] were walking on Venice Beach and just out of the blue he says, 'Hey do you want to play *Dungeons & Dragons*?'" Kyle said. "I instantly got really excited." Kyle texted his wife immediately, and the whole family was psyched to start a campaign. "It was a little bit too in the moment to get everything together to play right then and there." But they made plans to play a month later.

---

1. Shelly: She's definitely in my top three favorite lady villains, but I'm still scarred by the early illustrations of her. So disturbing, and yet I can't look away.

That's when Kyle jumped into the modern D&D community with two big feet. "I started listening to podcasts and started looking up what would be a good 1st-level adventure to DM these guys on," he said. He namechecks the *gg no re* podcast's vision of the Village of Hommlet and *Dice, Camera, Action* series with Chris Perkins DMing as a guide to the new edition of the rules.

"The thing that was just awesome about when we finally all got together— we played two nights in a row, about four hours each night—was just how immersed we all got into contributing to making this story," Kyle said about their first sessions. "Nobody was checking their phones. Nobody was doing anything except being completely in present time. . . . We had a blast."

That's just when they first started. Their games have leveled up significantly since then now that they play with some people from Illumination. The gaming style that Kyle and his wife, Janet, have developed over time is one that seriously feels like #CoupleGoals for me and Shelly to aim for with our spouses.

"My wife and I are co-DMing. She got really into effects and got a bunch of dry ice and strobe lights, trying to go all out in making props and all that," he told us. "She's in charge of ambience . . . I'm the frontline, telling the players what's happening. But whenever they encounter an NPC, Janet will play the women, and I'll do the men. It's funny cause we play off each other, and we interact with the players." It's also cool how she can add ambience he didn't explicitly design so she contributes to the whole table's immersion. "I'll be in the middle of telling a story and saying that they are entering a forest, and suddenly these forest sounds just [arrive]. It's great teamwork." If that doesn't bring up an image of Janet with headphones like a DJ spinning tracks for Kyle as DM, I don't know what's wrong with you.

So how does D&D relate to his career as a filmmaker? That's what Shelly and I really wanted to know. Do the two feel similar? Kyle was pretty clear about how the two disciplines are entwined so the skills learned or refined in one can affect the other. "*Dungeons & Dragons* is storytelling, it's so related to directing and DMing, there's a lot of crossover between those two things," he said. He talked about one example when running the *Death House* adventure: the party split up, and he as DM had to manage the player's attention carefully so as not to have one group be too bored when another is in the spotlight.

When that happened in the game he was DMing with his wife, they shared a quick look. "My wife and I looked at each and we were like, 'Okay we can do this,' in terms of the cross-cutting you have to do," he said with a laugh. "That is really like doing parallel action in film, when you split up and you are portraying different characters' [action] at the same time. Trying to read the group so you're following one person's story, and you're leading them through what's happening and they're telling you what they are doing, and trying to find a little bit of a cliffhanger. . . . And then you switch your attention to somebody else. So everybody wants to come back to their story too. [You're] just trying to keep the rooting interest and everyone involved in everyone else's story."

"It was so much fun. It was like real-time directing," Kyle said.

He said a few things during this interview describing this relationship between film and D&D that I'll never forget. Directing a film can feel like a rock band making a studio album—there are so many edits and layering of tracks that may have been recorded at various times over the past few months and trying to make the album perfect through nonstop iteration. DMing a story of *Dungeons & Dragons* is like that same rock band playing the material live in front of an audience. You are making that story real through performance.

"Aspiring screenwriters should play *Dungeons & Dragons*," said Kyle before Shelly and I asked if we could emblazon that quote on every billboard in L.A. "It's just a way to exercise that storytelling muscle."

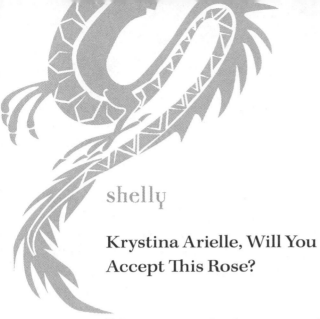

Krystina Arielle, Will You
Accept This Rose?

If I were to write this chapter using only emojis, it would be 1,600 smiley faces with heart eyes. Krystina is the Lisa Rinna to my Eileen Davidson. The Andy Cohen to my Anderson Cooper. The beautiful, long-stemmed, perfect rose to my starry-eyed, smitten Bachelorette. Yes, I will accept this rose.

It was 2018 when we first interviewed Krystina, an actor, cosplayer, and streamer. She was new to D&D, but quickly forged a reputation as one of the most entertaining and charismatic performers in the community. Her enthusiasm was contagious. Her (and my) love of reality television was not—to Greg. But he tolerated her waxing on about the *Real Housewives* more than he does for me so that tells you something.

All *Housewives* and *Bachelor* jokes aside, I had a really big revelation in this interview. I've spent years telling people anyone can (and should) play D&D. I love our beautiful, vibrant, diverse community. And I love running errands on a Saturday afternoon wearing a D&D T-shirt and surprising cashiers and baristas by regaling them with tales of my magical cat person alter ego. I wrote a book about a stereotypical girly girl's foray into roleplaying games and why everyone should feel welcome in this world, but when I'm in this world I don't always lead with the pedicures and reality TV and extensive collection of cocktail napkins emblazoned with pithy sayings about how much I don't like camping. I'm surrounded by some serious geeky people and sometimes wondered, "Can I love D&D and still choose a *House Hunters* marathon over *Lord of the Rings*?" Could D&D allow someone who isn't really a fantasy genre fan to play in this world? Would the D&D community accept my rose?

Unlike me, Krystina had some serious geek cred. She loved comic books and was a ginormous sci-fi and fantasy nerd and expert cosplayer. She was also an unapologetic lover of "trash TV" and celebrity gossip and somehow managed to wear both as well as her Lando Calrissian–inspired cosplay. (Her cosplay was so good it actually caught the attention of Billy Dee Williams!) I was free to be me! Or at least enticed by the idea of it.

You would never know Krystina isn't a lifelong D&D player given how well versed she is in rules and lore, but it is her passion that really stands out. She talked about the game with the same enthusiasm I had after surviving my intro to whitewater rafting on class IV rapids. (Except she continues to play D&D. My rafting career died on the same vine I tried to grab as our raft careened into a rocky cliffside.) The desire to play D&D had always been there for Krystina, but growing up a "Black nerd" in Georgia presented a lot of obstacles. People told her she couldn't play D&D. It wasn't for people like her. In the deep South, summoning demons in your living room was generally frowned upon.

You know how sometimes the universe really wants you to follow a path so it drops all sorts of hints at your feet until you finally notice and end up in exactly the place you were meant to be? The universe desperately wanted Krystina to pack up her car with all of her belongings, make the cross-country trek to Los Angeles, and get cast on the *Real Housewives of Beverly Hills*, and demand her new friend Shelly comes along too. (It's me. I'm the universe.) Really Krystina's goal was much simpler: land one great sci-fi role that would allow her to cosplay on the convention circuit for the rest of her life. After only a month on the West Coast, she met her now husband and was engaged a year later. Then she met Xander Jeanneret and Bonnie Gordon from the nerd song parody group the Library Bards and got a peek into the giant nerd portal. You might think Southern California is known for theme parks and In-N-Out Burger, but nope. It's all about a robust and supportive gaming community, composed of very talented creative types. She started watching shows like *Critical Role* and thought, "I can do that," but still had no idea how to actually do that. Besides, D&D wasn't for her. So she put D&D on the back burner and continued watching trashy TV shows and working on her more socially acceptable cosplay hobby.

Again, because the universe knew Krystina was exactly the kind of person who belonged in the *Dungeons & Dragons* community, she was invited to play D&D with the all-bard cast of *Sirens of the Realms*, thus finally granting Krystina's wish to play D&D. Of course, there was a small catch. Her first time rolling dice would be on stream. As in *live*. As in with an audience. Of course, Krystina didn't actually think of it as a "catch" and embraced the opportunity because that's what you do when you're a real-life bard.

To prepare for her first game, Krystina read everything she could about D&D, watched other live-streams, listened to podcasts, and basically "went ham on all things D&D." Speaking of podcasts, she used to listen to *Dragon Talk* in the car with her oldest son. He would sometimes share nuggets he learned from "Lore You Should Know" with other kids on the playground. When she told him she was going to be our guest, he said she wasn't famous enough for *Dragon Talk*. Well, kid, I have news for you!

The character she brought to the *Sirens* table was Orisha, an Aasimar 5th-level cleric/2nd-level bard or rather, "the imagined Krystina." Orisha spontaneously knocked out musical numbers as a diversionary tactic. She even burst into song during our interview, mesmerizing Greg and me with a ballad so enchanting, we didn't even notice it was about murder. Naturally I had to request "Money Can't Buy You Class" by Countess Luann, and she nailed that too. But this was where things skidded off the rails faster than the countess herself drunkenly skidding off a porch in Mexico and falling into the bushes. The D&D talk was fun, but I had many burning questions that needed answering:

- Who in their right mind would trust Ramona?
- What was up with Erika Jayne's red latex top and black mini-skirt in Berlin? How funny was it when she was almost run over by a bicyclist?
- True or false? *The Real Housewives of Potomac* is by far the most underrated franchise.

Poor Greg had to sit there confused and frightened that he might be called on, much like me when he and our other guests got all moony about *Princess Bride*, Star Trek, or musical theater. When he tried to join in, we berated him for not knowing which franchise we were talking about. It was Lisa Rinna who threw the wine glass at Kim Richards! Come on, Greg! This was a classic scene!

We did manage to bring the conversation back to D&D—sort of. Krystina had this amazing idea to bring her two favorite hobbies together for some epic entertainment—a *Housewives*-themed roleplaying game. Honestly, I think it's brilliant. First, instead of a Dungeon Master you play the role of "producer" and your job is to squeeze out the most drama from the other players. Everyone has a trigger word or phrase ("Bully," "Take a Xanax!," "Be cool, don't be all uncool"), and when you discover someone's hot button, you get points for riling them up. You roll for drama instead of dexterity, but there's no saving throw for getting caught in it. There could be tables that determine what the Housewives were fighting over like:

- Someone planted a story in *Page Six* about how you threw a butter knife at one of your costars after she accused you of wearing a Fendi knock-off.
- Someone suggested your child looks a lot like someone else's husband.
- Someone accused you of having "pretend amnesia."
- Someone pours a healing potion in a champagne flute when clearly it goes in a wine glass. How uncouth!

Every player gets three "really's?" to use at their discretion, but on the third "really?" you roll for initiative. We all loved the idea of confessionals or diary rooms, for any D&D game really, especially if your character has a secret subplot the other players don't know about.

Are we funding this game or what?

If you like that idea, wait until you hear about the *Real Housewives of Faerûn* series we keep threatening to make.

Time flew and when the interview was over, I was beaming. There is no bond like a Bravo TV bond.

A year later I was on my way to D&D Live 2019: The Descent in Los Angeles. D&D Live was becoming our mega-event of the year with a mix of D&D–loving celebs, streamers, podcasters, and aficionados coming together for a weekend of panels and gaming. It felt like returning to summer camp. I was thrilled to be attending but not because I had a hotel room and room service and was kid-free. The real draw was meeting Krystina in real life. We had spent the past year expressing our hopes and dreams for the day we would finally come face to come. Not gonna lie, I was more nervous than a Housewife on reunion day. What if I wasn't as articulate as the GIFs I sent her on Twitter? What if she didn't recognize me? What if she liked her geekier friends better?

Not to blow things out of proportion or blur facts with hyperbole, but our IRL meeting was something out of a Nancy Meyers movie. Picture me, coming in hot and sweaty from the airport, barely out of the Uber, tripping over my carry-on bag in my excitement. The first thirty people I saw all said something like, "Krystina is looking for you!" or "OMG did you know Krystina is *here?*" or "Did you seriously just run right past your husband you haven't seen in three days and into Krystina's arms?" (I sure did!) I pushed through the crowd gathered in the parking lot and like a beautiful unicorn encased in a sunbeam, I saw her holding court in front of the gourmet grilled cheese food truck. A Black nerd from Georgia who was discouraged from playing D&D was the belle of the ball. Seas of attendees clad in D&D ampersand T-shirts hushed as two hurtling comets prepared to crash into each other. Okay, it's been a few years, but that's how I remember it. After a long embrace, we launched into a deep discussion about *90 Day Fiancé*.

Since that *Dragon Talk* interview, things changed for Krystina and me. She has appeared in numerous D&D streams including *Critical Role*, Dimension 20's *Pirates of Leviathan*, and *Into the Mother Lands* RPG; had a second appearance on *Dragon Talk*; and is currently the host of *Star Wars: The High Republic*. Not too shabby for a girl who didn't feel like she belonged in the geek community. I have managed to bring up my love of *The Bachelor* in every team meeting and make a *Real Housewives* reference in almost every episode of *Dragon Talk*. I bring my subscription copies of *Us Weekly* into the company gym and admit when I don't get the joke because I haven't seen *Loki* or *The Witcher* (but you know I binged the latest season of *Selling Sunset* as soon as it was released), and I just shrug when my coworkers squeal in disbelief. But guess what? They still talk to me, even when it's not required for their job. In fact, a few unexpected ones have outed themselves as *Bachelor* fans too. Maybe I have inspired them. She may not be a Dungeon Master (yet), but Krystina sure knew how to give out inspiration.

greg

Battling Demons IRL
with Michael Mallen the Id DM

Content warning: Depression, suicide

T his was a tough one.

Shelly and I knew it was going to be a hard subject to discuss with Michael Mallen since his brother had died by suicide only two years before our interview. Michael wanted to be a hero in the community as an advocate for mental health beyond his profession as a licensed psychologist. He wanted to candidly talk about his brother's depression on *Dragon Talk* because he thought it was important to remove the stigma around suicide and discuss ways to help those who are suffering. We hadn't necessarily shied away from mentioning serious subjects on the podcast before, but it was another thing altogether to concentrate an entire interview on talking about something that was obviously still so raw for Michael.

But that was kind of Michael's whole point. People being uncomfortable talking to him about his brother's death was the exact thing he wanted us all to get over already. Not talking about it had the potential to cause far more harm than ignoring it out of misguided politeness. So we decided to confront our own demons and hear what he had to say because we thought it was important for the D&D community to recognize folks who are hurting at your table and potentially reach out to them.

By the time we spoke to him in 2019, Michael had been a part of the D&D community for more than decade. In the late 2000s and early 2010s, D&D discourse online was ruled by bloggers with handles using the "_____ DM" format.[1] "I had created that account back in the fourth edition days when everyone was 'The Something DM,'" he said. He chose "The Id DM" as his moniker online because it was (A) short enough to help with Twitter's character counts; (B) no one had taken it yet, so Twitter, WordPress, and his email could all match; and (C) "if you say it quick it sounds like 'idiom,' which I liked. Reminds me of Monty Python for some reason," he said.

On the *Id DM* blog, he wrote articles about monsters or spells or group dynamics or basically anything about running a D&D fourth edition game. Michael also runs his own podcast, *Ego Check*, which I was grateful to be a guest on early in my tenure at Wizards. He discusses a wide range of topics, but there's a concentration on gaming and mental health.

All that is basically due to his brother introducing him to D&D while growing up in New Jersey in the 1980s. "My older brother and his friends were very much into sports," Michael said. But there were some in that crew who weren't just jocks. They were more like the character of Billy in *Stranger Things*. "Some of his friends were that guy who was into hard rock, metal music, listened to Iron Maiden, and was just a very interesting characters.

"But they also played D&D," he said. "Sometimes they would play D&D in our den. I was five years younger than my brother and I always wanted to get in the game. And of course, they were like, 'No, get out of here kid. You're not allowed to play.'" Being an annoying ten-year-old little brother at the time (something I can totally relate to since I definitely exhibited little sibling energy around this same timeframe), he just kept asking and asking until they finally relented.

Little Michael rolled up a basic level 1 fighter. He was so excited to be able to play with the cool kids! His first combat came quickly. The party was attacked by a monster in a cave, and his fighter ran up to swing his sword. Then the ranger threw a flask of oil at the monster, dousing both combatants, before another tossed a lit torch on the spilled oil. If you can see where this is going, then you are smarter than little Michael was, sadly. "Everything goes up in flames, including me," Michael said. "And I die. That quickly."

"I think I got to play for about fifteen minutes." The older teens said, "You

---

1. Greg: Such as my friends Philippe-Antoine Ménard, "ChattyDM," or Enrique Bertran, "NewbieDM."

can sit and watch." Which seemed like exactly what they were trying to accomplish, showing Michael that this just wasn't a kid's game.

Some people would take that experience pretty terribly. What the older kids did to Michael was not cool, and nine times out of ten it would push anyone out of ever wanting to play D&D again. But instead of pushing him away, it made him want to play the game even more and, perhaps, be better prepared. "It didn't traumatize me for life," Michael said, I think as a joke, but this phrase stuck with me given the context of this interview.

Michael told us during this interview that his father was killed in the line of duty as a police officer in New Jersey when he was eight years old and his brother was thirteen. The two of them dealt with that shared trauma very differently. "We had such an intense relationship," he said. "We went through that traumatic experience together as a family. I think—I know—that made me look up to him as a father figure."

I may be inserting some narrative here, but it seems like Michael's brother channeled some of that trauma into his drive to succeed as an athlete. He was the star quarterback of the high school football team. He had the adoration of his peers and was on top of the world, if teen comedy movies from the 1980s are to be believed. Colleges heavily recruited him out of high school and he was poised to lead a glorious, successful life.

Meanwhile, Michael's love of gaming, D&D, and nerdy things grew in his teens. He was inspired to help others deal with the emotional ups and downs of life, and combined with his skill with math and other academics, he worked hard in college and grad school to become a psychologist. He jumped back into the D&D fandom he loved as a kid when the fourth edition was published in 2007, started playing regularly again, and eventually channeled that into his blog writing.

His brother didn't fare so well. The football experience at college wasn't quite Heisman Trophy–winning material. He returned to the hometown that had once adored him and became a fixture in the community as a firefighter. He married and raised a family, and was very well liked by pretty much everyone in town. But even after a few decades had passed from when he was young, he couldn't shake the feeling that he had somehow failed. He didn't live up to the expectations he had set for himself, and that wasn't all he was experiencing.

"During that time he was exposed to a lot of traumatic situations. Car accidents, fires. He was in the recovery efforts for 9/11 afterward," Michael said.

"More first responders, especially firefighters, are dying by suicide rather than the line-of-duty deaths, because of the grind, the emotional toll that comes with that profession."

Then a few life changes were thrown in his brother's path. "He was going through some marriage issues, some things at work changed, his schedule changed. There were numerous stressors that were loaded onto his plate over the span of eighteen months," Michael said. "It was one thing after the other."

In June 2017, Michael's brother ended his life.

It's even harder for Michael to talk about this because he recognized changes in his brother but wasn't able to prevent what happened. "Being a psychologist and being his brother, I was aware that he was 'not himself.' He was sort of withdrawn," he said. "And I spoke to him a few months before he died about suicide. I asked about it directly. I expressed concern for him. I wish I could remember exactly how that conversation went. He felt alone, but he wasn't alone."

That's the crux of what Michael wanted to get across by talking to us. You are not alone. Everyone is going through the same shit life throws at you on this adventure we call life. Whether it's your family, your gaming group, or a professional like Michael, it's important to talk through what you are feeling. If you observe behaviors like being withdrawn or pulling away from stuff they used to love, even those behaviors in people who you think have "made it," don't hesitate to reach out to them and help them get help.

"Somebody can have the perfect job, or the perfect family, or the perfect whatever," he said. "It doesn't have anything to do with that." You can be the star quarterback, the rock star, the beloved comedian, or a D&D podcast host and still feel alone and depressed and consider suicide. "We're all suffering."

I am not exempt from these feelings. As I write this, I'm no longer experiencing depression, but I wasn't so sure of that back in 2019 when I was talking to Michael at Shelly's house. For a variety of reasons mostly made up by my brain, I was convinced I was a piece of shit. It's only through reflection under the lens Michael offers here that I can consider the good that's in my life. I now make a choice to try to shine the light on others so they can feel proud of their accomplishments as much as I can. Lift you up!

Michael's brother didn't feel like he was important, but the sad truth is that he meant something to many people in that town in New Jersey: mothers he saved from burning buildings, kids who got their pets back from his ladder unit, or men whose lives he saved from a car wreck; heck, even peers who loved having a winning football team at their school when he was young. They all looked up to him.

"We had a service for my brother after he died and—I'm not exaggerating —a few thousand people came through for hours [to pay their respects]," he said. His brother's death was on the front page of the local newspaper. Despite all those people who might have been available to help him, Michael's brother still felt alone.

"There are thousands of my brother out there," Michael said. "Everybody we walk past during the day has something going on. They are all struggling with something.

"It doesn't choose," he said.

I chose this topic to discuss on a *Dungeons & Dragons* podcast for exactly that reason. I had seen the community—or at least the parts that I pay close attention to on Twitter—openly talk about their bad days. They celebrated their wins and when they felt proud, sure, but I was touched by the openness some folks had in showing their emotions and letting others know there are people like them experiencing these feelings too. It's a testament to how much roleplaying and emotional storytelling in this game can make a real difference in how gamers consider their own life and their own roles. For some, playing a game like D&D is an escape from the pain. For others, it opens a doorway to communication to your psyche in ways you never thought possible before.

Like coming onto the *Dungeons & Dragons* podcast to raise money for a good cause. That's how Michael Mallen chose to invest his energy and time. After his brother's death, he came on to tell us about a project called No Assembly Required, a PDF full of monsters for use in D&D with sales proceeds going to the American Foundation for Suicide Prevention. To date, Michael has raised more than $5,000 for that foundation from the D&D community.

More than that, he's broken down the barriers and social stigma around suicidal thoughts and let us all know how to be here for each other like every good D&D party should be.

Finding the Fun with Xander Jeanneret

You may know Xander Jeanneret as half of the nerd parody group the Library Bards, a professional roleplayer who has appeared in popular live-action roleplay series like *Relics & Rarities* and *Dark Lanterns*, and a season two contestant on the reality competition show *King of the Nerds* (which puts me fourteen degrees from a Real Housewife). But what he should be most known for is convincing his mom, aunt, and their friends to play D&D and broadcasting it to the whole world.

Moms are pretty much the best people. I was blessed with one who fully believed everything I did was brilliant and deserved attention. (A lot of things about me make sense now, right?) She kept all my short stories, programs from high school plays, even my Presidential Fitness Award because of course Ronald Regan singled me out for my outstanding ability to perform thirteen partial curl-ups in two minutes. I had no idea how much I needed moms playing D&D until I read an article and watched a video recapping Xander's mother-of-all-D&D experience. A few years before, I indoctrinated my own mom into the world of dungeon delving and it went . . . well, differently.

As proud as she was that her baby wrote a how-to book (and apologies to the Barnes & Noble staff who had to remove my book from various endcaps every time she shopped there), my mom still couldn't explain *Dungeons & Dragons*.

"It's about dungeons *and* dragons!

"It's a board game where everyone pretends to be wizards!

"Oh, you know, just look for a game called *Dungeons & Dragons*. Maybe it's on the computer?

"Umm, you kill dragons and collect money and the first one to get out of the dungeon becomes the Dungeon Master."

There was no denying it: my mom didn't read my book. When confronted, she did her best to deny it. "Of course I did! I just didn't understand all the fantasy references."

"I referenced Oprah and Jimmy Choo shoes," I sighed.

"Well, it got very complicated. I may have skimmed it looking for my name. I loved the illustrations though."

What choice did I have? I couldn't censor her delusional exploitation of her child's accomplishments, but I also couldn't have her out there misrepresenting the good word of D&D. Who knew how else she was describing our beloved game? So one summer night while I was home on vacation, I poured three large glasses of wine, lured my parents out to the patio, and surprised them with the *Dungeons & Dragons Starter Set.*

"Tonight, you are adventurers," I said. "Tonight, you learn how to play *Dungeons & Dragons.*"

"Oh no, please," she said. "I'll read the book. I promise."

"But the Yankees are on," my dad said, wondering how he got roped into this. He was always honest about not reading my book.

When they realized I wasn't going away, my dad agreed to play only if he could be a pirate, and my mom grudgingly accepted her role as a dwarf fighter. "Grudgingly" for about twenty-three seconds. Once she understood there was no board or fake money and she could try anything she desired, she ransacked the tavern, stole money from the barkeep, took down a bunch of drunk goblins with a spinning kick, and scared the crap out of my dad.

"I don't like what this game is doing to your mother," he said.

"Can I hit him too?" she asked, nodding in my dad's direction. "I don't like his attitude."

"No, you can't," I explained. I mean, she could, but sometimes Dungeon Masters lie to protect their fathers. "You're on the same team. You're supposed to help each other."

We played long enough for them both to get it. My dad, pirate or not, would probably never play again, but I always suspected my mom would have given it another go.

With Xander, we covered lots of great topics like how there's no jealousy among D&D content creators, the safe space roleplaying games provide, *Schitt's Creek,* and the concept of bleed, where in-game emotions seep into your real-world self. This can be good or bad depending on what happened in the story. If a character experiences trauma, the player might find themselves feeling anxious or depressed in real life. Conversely, if the party staged an epic coup and emerged victorious, the players might carry feelings of euphoria into their everyday work. This comes up a lot in our discussions about D&D.

To know Xander is to love him, and to love him means not being able to say no to him, which is how he got these sweet, grown-up, Midwest women to let him record their first foray into *Dungeons & Dragons*. Turns out Xander has a history of encouraging people to play D&D with him. When he was in fifth grade, he used his birthday as an excuse to encourage his friends to play. One of them had to step up and be the Dungeon Master because Xander wanted to be a player! Can't say no to the birthday boy, right?

As a theater major in college, he was surrounded by friends who actually wanted to play D&D with him. Like any good theater kid, he left college with a degree in delusion and headed off to L.A. to become an actor, because that's how it works. But unlike most theater majors (okay, me), he was successful. He quickly fell into the L.A. nerd community and caught the attention of producers from Geek and Sundry and the Nerdist.

What makes Xander so universally loved is his "find the fun" philosophy about character creation and Dungeon Mastering (and I suspect life in general). His *Dark Lanterns* character was a Mark of Healing halfling named Waltz,[1] who was an exotic dancer who manifested his powers and expressed himself with dance. His signature move was Flying Silk, and it involved mage hand holding one end of the scarf he wore around his waist and twirling him like a top. The result was a beautifully choreographed execution of divine silky entanglement for his opponents. It was at this point in the interview I admitted that I thought he said Waltz was an *erotic* dancer who was working it to get those powers. (Also a good backstory. No judgment here!)

"Gives new meaning to *Magic* Mike," Greg said.

"*Magic Mike XXS*," Xander added, "Because he was a halfling."

Back to the midwestern moms who melted my heart. While visiting Wisconsin for vacation, Xander thought it would be fun to stream a game with

---

1. Shelly: Halflings are a diminutive, friendly player race who get along with pretty much everyone. A Mark of Healing is a halfling trait allowing the character to heal or even save a life with a touch.

his mother and her sister, but before they even started, his instincts told him it could be bigger. He called Greg and pitched the idea of "piercing the veil" of RPGs for his mom so she would finally understand what was happening at young Xander's birthday parties when she snuck downstairs to make sure everyone had enough chips and punch all those years ago. Greg was sold, loving the idea of parents diving into their kids' geeky hobbies to understand what they're so passionate about. The party grew to include Xander's aunt and friends. He may have told the ladies if they didn't allow Xander to teach them and record the whole thing, Greg would never let him play D&D again. Greg is very powerful like that.

The moms were not required to dress in a costume or use a funny accent, but that's what they saw Xander do, so they wanted to as well. For them, horned helmets and faux fur vests were "where to find the fun." They may not have fully understood the rules, but they definitely got their characters.

Before that day, their collective D&D knowledge could fill a halfling's boot. One thought it was a video game, one thought it involved "hanging out," and another thought D&D stood for designated driver. I mean, it also does, but that's not as fun.

Their pending fantastical adventure began as anything but.

"You are mothers," Xander begins.

You cannot shake your kids, even in a realm far, far away.

". . . of acclaimed adventurers that have come down with a deadly disease."

There was a cure, but they had to find all the ingredients and bring them to a potion master.

"The first ingredient," Xander tells the group, "was the hair of a unicorn."

The moms set off to cure their children, but Xander's mom quickly tired of all the looking and talking. She was a fighter! She was skilled in intimidation. She wanted to throw some punches, not perceive things! She and my mom would have made a feisty adventuring duo.

"Everything's so nice and pretty," she complained. "There's no one to fight yet!"

Xander assured her the time would come to put those skills to use.

Their search for the unicorn hair gave them more adventure than they bargained for. They discovered LaRue the Unicorn was in grave danger and needed their help. How do you say no to helping a unicorn if they promise to give you some of their hair in return? This is the moment with new players I love—when it all clicks. They forget there are rules, forget the nerves, forget they're playing a game. They become real heroes on a quest to find mysterious ingredients in hopes a potion master can devise an antidote to save their poisoned children, and if they happen to save a hunted unicorn along the way, all the better. Fully immersed in the game and their characters, they plotted with each other. They compared notes and theories. They thought they saw the group threatening LaRue and knew where they were.

"Are you going there?" Xander asked.

"Damn straight we are!"

Spoiler: they killed the bad guys and saved LaRue. The healer was so committed to doing the right thing she wouldn't hurt anyone. Xander's mom, however, was chomping at the bit to get in there. She even got a crit and decapitated a wolf. The ladies applauded, congratulated each other, and reached across the table to toast their victory.

Xander admitted he didn't know what would happen. He knew them in real life but could only imagine who their fantasy selves were. The women went in with zero expectations. They couldn't have guessed where their adventure would take them. Most surprising was perhaps how they felt after.

"Everything was so detailed, it made me feel like a child again."

"I can't wait for it to go on!"

"It's beyond what I could have imagined."

They realized that D&D was a story of different people from different backgrounds told by different people with different backgrounds. Sadly, they didn't get a chance to play together again, but I guarantee they're no longer telling strangers you win D&D by defeating everyone else and becoming the Dungeon Master. Anyone can play D&D. Everyone *should*. At least according to Xander's mom.

"Get in there and play it!" she advised. "Don't just be the mom with the food!"

Listen to your mother, kids. And roll some dice with her too.

Greg

Adrienne Palmer Jumps
Off the Top Rope

The artist formerly known as Ember Moon inspires us all to make our dreams become reality.

I'm not just talking about playing D&D in a professional setting, like she does on the YouTube show *Roll Out* or in *Acquisitions Incorporated* at PAX. In our interview from July 2019, Adrienne Palmer told us that she decided early in her life that she wanted to be a professional wrestler and worked as hard as she could to achieve her goal as she became an adult. Discovering D&D while she was working semi-professionally as a wrestler helped keep those dreams on track with some well-needed escapism, and maybe a little inspiration from the game infected her professional life.

That's right—the character of Ember Moon was loosely based on a dark elf fighter mage character she played in second edition AD&D.[1] The powers that be at WWE didn't think she could get away with using swords and banners in the ring like the D&D character she pitched to them, but they latched on to the darker persona in her first promo videos. They even digitally added the color red into her eyes in those videos. When it was ready for her debut in 2007, Adrienne embraced it all and bought red contact lenses to wear in the ring. Ember Moon was born!

Quick note about professional wrestling in the United States for those of you reading who may not be familiar with elbow drops, body slams, and the intricacies of folding chair combat. While the presentation may resemble

---

1. Greg: Dark elves, otherwise known as drow, have a complicated history with Black people (see the essay with Tanya DePass), but it was cool to hear about Ember having a positive experience playing one of them all the way back in the 1990s.

a heightened version of other professional sports like basketball or soccer, wrestling as portrayed in leagues like the WWE (World Wrestling Entertainment) is more like a dramatic performance with the combatants taking on larger-than-life personas. These performers tell a story that unfolds in the ring through intricate matches using staged combat maneuvers and in interactions on camera through interviews and a social media presence. Ember Moon is not her real name or even her real persona, and the costume and personality are crafted in collaboration with the league. That doesn't sound too far off from a DM working with a player on their character's backstory, does it?

But we're getting ahead of ourselves. Let's go back to the start, with Adrienne as a kid. Like many of us—including Shelly and me—Adrienne told us she was bullied by other girls in middle school because she was different. She dared to wear Barney T-shirts and read comic books and other stuff that was determined to be super gross by the queen bee bitches of her school.[2]

Young Adrienne wasn't a fighter yet, and she didn't have much recourse until she found her partner in crime, another girl who defended her and took them all out with a vicious leg sweep before following up with a massive uppercut to the face. Oh wait, that was the fantasy. In real life, she ended up just as terrorized as Adrienne by the mean girls. But at least she had a friend. As if it was destined by a sage of the Forgotten Realms, this friend was a huge fan of professional wrestling.

The power fantasy began slowly. Adrienne and her friend would get together after school and watch the wrestlers of the time, like Triple H and Stephanie McMahon. They'd say to each other, "We're going to become wrestlers so we can defend ourselves and stand up for ourselves." They even came up with their own personas, saying, "We're going to do this to them!" as they mimicked the moves they saw on TV. The bullying was so intimidating that all this pretending to be badass was just a fantasy. When they saw the mean girls in the halls the next day, the courage of their pretend personas melted away into meekness once again. Middle school was hard, y'all.

High school and hormones changed the landscape for Adrienne. She wasn't bullied anymore, and her parents encouraged her to get into soccer to supplement her good grades so she would be accepted at a good university on a scholarship. "For years, it was soccer and school, soccer and school. Soccer

2. Greg: "Queen bee bitches" was her phrase, not mine, I think.

will get you into a good school, so you play soccer. Soccer, soccer, soccer, school, school, school." But the rebelliousness of wrestling was always there in the background, and Adrienne started thinking about selecting a college that was close to a wrestling training gym. None of that worked out, since financial aid didn't arrive as expected, and she enrolled at a community college. As fate would have it, though, a small wrestling gym opened up around the corner from her campus and, still holding on to the fantasy, she joined the gym unbeknownst to her parents.

It really was a heroine's journey for Adrienne. That first gym was in a super tiny space. "The ring was fifteen feet by fifteen feet, and the building was sixteen feet wide," she said. Which meant any time the trainees needed to bounce off the elastic ropes, they made indentations into the walls of the gym with their rumps. "You had to run the ropes in a certain spot or else you would be hitting the wall. There was also no air conditioning." She told this to the whippersnappers coming up in WWE like a veteran—"Back in my day we had no AC!" They all called her Auntie Ember, perhaps deservedly so, but that makes her sound like an awesome hag NPC. We'll get to that!

She kept her wrestling secret from her parents while she was in college. It was the first time she had done something for herself, and she didn't want their judgment until she had determined whether it was going to work out. I can relate—D&D was a pastime my parents definitely discouraged, and it wasn't until I made the choice to do it anyway that this whole weird career opened up to me. You don't have to ask your parents if it's okay to pursue your dreams, you know? In some way, crossing that threshold is what makes us adults and Adrienne took that step by training in the little gym and telling her parents she was up late studying.

"I was going to college, working two jobs, and by night I was a vigilante wrestler," she joked. The training went well, and she started performing in local wrestling events. That's where her love of D&D began. A friend of her boyfriend (now husband) suggested they learn to play together, and after a bit of reluctance from Adrienne—this was when D&D had a bit of a social stigma associated with it—she tried it out and never looked back.

After wrestling events or when they didn't have stuff booked, a group would get together and roll dice. The adventuring party could include another wrestler or a friend of a friend of a wrestler, or someone who worked concessions at the event, or an announcer, or whoever showed up. "We played with everyone who wanted to jump in and have an experience." It was the complete D&D experience, indeed, with Cheetos, THAC0, and a healthy amount of Mountain Dew. (This was the 1990s, after all.)

In Adrienne's first D&D session, she played a human cleric of Mystra. Because it was a previous version of the game, the initiative roll was based on the weapon wielded, and her cleric had a slow-ass flail.[3] This was unfortunate because, perhaps as belied by her chosen profession, she just wanted to beat things up in D&D. "I remember having many a temper tantrum of running out of spells and not being able to do anything," she said. That first session is the source of "so much anger toward being the healer. I want to hit things really fast. I don't want people to depend on me." In the next game, she played a wizard who "accidentally" *fireball*ed the bad guys and some of her party in the process.[4] "They got a little toasty," she admitted.

One of the fantastic parts of her D&D fandom is how it's an activity she and her husband love to do. He was instrumental in getting her into that first game, and they still play actively. Shelly asked if Adrienne enjoys playing with her husband, while mentioning she didn't necessarily like playing with her own partner and often gets annoyed at the parts of his personality that show up at the table. (Sorry, Bart.) Adrienne said that, if anything, she probably annoyed *her* partner with her instigating ways.

Example: while sneaking into a hag's lair in a recent *Curse of Strahd* session,[5] Adrienne's character came upon a barrel filled with an opaque liquid. Not wanting to leave any barrel unturned, she immediately pushed it over to make sure there wasn't something important hidden inside. Of course, crashing a barrel to the ground isn't exactly stealthy, and her blundering alerted all three of the hags, instead of following her husband's plan to take them out one by one. "He gets so upset at me making terrible D&D decisions," she laughed.

---

3. Greg: Rolling initiative determines which characters are able to act on their turn before the others. It's an imperfect abstraction of how chaotic actions take place on the battlefield, but it works.

4. Greg: *Fireball* is an iconic D&D move/spell that kind of does what it says on the tin. A ball of fire erupts and does fire damage to anyone (friend or foe) in the blast. It's spawned many a meme with a variation of the caption "When you absolutely, positively have to kill every mother****** in the room."

5. Greg: *Curse of Strahd* is a vampire-themed adventure released in 2016. It's funny how nearly everyone we talk to on *Dragon Talk* recently has played a version of this adventure.

As Adrienne's love of D&D grew, so did her wrestling career. In 2007, WWE offered her a chance to work with arguably the biggest sports entertainment franchises out there, and her character was introduced to the world as part of the NXT brand. She used that success to fund her love of D&D with a game room in their house, and she made sure to help younger wrestlers understand that you have to work hard to make your dreams come true, even if destiny can help out a little bit.

Remember her friend who liked wrestling back when they were fending off the queen bees of middle school? Like many young friendships, the two eventually lost touch. While Adrienne pursued their shared dream of wrestling, the friend went on to other pursuits. They had lost contact for a few years, but she reached out to an old email address of Adrienne's and fate intervened there too!

Out of the blue, she sent an email to Adrienne with a message wondering if the address was still working. "It's crazy. It feels like it was fate that we were supposed to be reunited," Adrienne said, since she was only logging into that old address because it was connected to an old device. She hadn't touched it for years. "Literally I think she had sent it a minute before I logged in. And I was like, 'Whoa, this is creepy.'"

Now they talk whenever they can with Adrienne's busy schedule, and her friend couldn't believe that the dream they had together back when they were kids had actually come true. But that's just what Adrienne does.

In one very tiny and honestly inconsequential way, Adrienne inspired me to get out there and make a tiny dream of mine a reality. When we interviewed her, she was in her D&D game room in her home. There were castles and dragon skulls and miniatures in the background, and it was awesome to behold a professional adult with the daring to carve out a space of their own for their favorite pastime. It still is their favorite thing to do. Adrienne and her husband play regularly, and she's on record as saying she wants to play *Curse of Strahd* or *Ravenloft* every year for the rest of her life.

Her descriptions of her game room inspired me to carve out a space in my family's new home. My wife and I had been eternal renters since we got a first janky apartment together in 2000, and we've moved around the country a lot. We were finally able to lay down some roots in the Seattle area and buy a house in late 2019. One of the biggest selling points for me was that I'd be able to place all my D&D books, miniatures, and nerdery into one amazing game room. My daughters and I use it to play chess, family friends come over to play pinochle, and, of course, I DMed more than a few games before the pandemic hit. It's become the background to all my Zoom calls, meetings, and podcast recordings over the last year and a makeshift studio for my online D&D sessions, complete with lights, cameras, and scenery!

I may not have made all that happen without Adrienne's inspiration. Because our interview was so inspiring, Shelly asked near the end if she ever considered teaching young people about wrestling. She's thought a lot about becoming Auntie Ember for real (not the hag) and more formally training the next generation of sports entertainment professionals. But she's got more to do before that happens.

"It's always been my dream to open a school . . . to train people to do what I love," she said. "But that's years down the road since there's so much more I want to learn personally before that."

As for her future as a wrestler and a creator, the sky is wide open. Adrienne was released from her contract with WWE in November 2021. She's independent now and can pursue all these dreams on her own terms.

Gaming and Growing with
Adam Johns and Adam Davis

In college, my friend Kathy and I had a passion for music and by that I mean, putting on our finest flannel, pooling the money we made recycling beer cans, and going to bars to listen to bands. Neither of us were musically inclined, but we were average theater majors savvy enough to know we'd probably need more realistic career paths. To that end, we decided that after graduation, we'd move to New York City and get jobs scouting bands for major labels, but still have time to take the occasional speaking role on my favorite soap operas. Delusion is the Miracle-Gro of unattainable dreams.

We did none of these things.

Adam Johns and Adam Davis met in college and were a bit more pragmatic in their future planning. Both were studying family and drama therapy and happened to be avid roleplayers. Because they also happened to be savvy, educated, do-gooders, they recognized early on the many therapeutic benefits their favorite pastime had to offer.

In 2013, the Adams (as they shall be known henceforth) founded Wheelhouse Workshop, an organization that provided therapeutic social skills for teenagers using *Dungeons & Dragons*. I'm pretty sure I spent the whole interview with a tear beading down my cheek. Every time I played D&D after meeting the Adams, I thought about the kids and adults in their group who were gaining valuable skills and improving the quality of their lives. The Adams were able to give their clients something many people take for granted: friendships. Making and keeping friends might be something you've done your whole life. For others, it's a woefully undeveloped skill.

Normally, I'd say I'm outgoing, love hosting gatherings, and count myself lucky to have a good group of close friends. But after nearly two years of quar-antining, I've changed. I was either way too chatty around strangers ("Why are you leaving so soon, nice pizza man?") or shy, awkward, and confused ("Where does this gas pump gooooooooooooo?"). Obviously, my social skills might be a bit rusty, but I'm fairly confident they'll come back. There's got to be some muscle memory there, right?

What happens if you never mastered the art of small talk, introducing yourself, or fostering a blossoming friendship? Kids can be open-minded and get attached quickly. "You like LEGO? I do too. Let's build LEGO rocket ships side by side forever." But they can also sniff out when someone's different, and at a certain age, "different" can be hard to recover from.

Enter Wheelhouse Workshop and the Adams who, like Dr. Megan, act as "therapeutic Dungeon Masters." Wheelhouse started in 2013, but the Adams were already dabbling in "applied D&D" with another organization before they took over Wheelhouse. They were leading an improv group around the same time and carried over a lot of skills like spontaneity, flexibility, and lis-tening to Dungeon Mastering. With applied D&D, they were creating custom mini games within D&D games tailored to meet their clients' needs.

At the time of the interview, the Adams were running five weekly D&D groups for thirty kids (and sometimes adults) ranging in age from nine to twenty-four. Some of their clients were people with Asperger syndrome, ADHD, or anxiety, although a doctor's note was not required to join the group. Some of the biggest hurdles these kids faced was having difficulty making friends, getting along with peers, or finding ways to be interested in other people's interests. D&D was a great teaching tool because collaboration was key to success. After a group brainstorm, sometimes the Adams had the kids vote on which ideas are best, allowing them to recognize achievements outside of themselves.

Even though they're therapists, the Adams say they're more like Mr. Mi-yagi from *The Karate Kid*. The customized games were often embedded with purposeful puzzles and plot points designed to teach kids basic social skills. Whatever area of growth the client needed to work on, they would see that mirrored in their character's development. The best part was they were doing this while having fun. Playing a game didn't feel like therapy, an important distinction when so many of these kids didn't fare well with traditional routes.

One example of how real-life therapy intersects fantasy world characters was early on they had a group trying to break into a goblin stronghold. The party was desperate to get in, but the goblins weren't having it. The wizard, a child who needed to overcome a challenge to feel successful, cast *tongues* and was able to speak to the goblins in their language. He was in the middle of a convincing story when one of the Adams made the spell run out. Unimpressed with the gibberish the wizard started spouting, the goblins were about to shut this party down for good. Out of options and unable to speak goblin, the player had the inspired idea to mime the rest of his story. This delighted the goblins (and the group), who allowed the whole party entry into the stronghold. The player was beaming with newfound confidence.

The Adams use pregen character sheets,[1] but there's still a lot of room for customization. They ask a lot of questions to help flesh out a character's backstory (Do you have siblings? Are you from a big or small town? Do you like to get up close in battle or stand far away?), all of which provided insights into where their clients were struggling the most. They encouraged us to think about our past characters and what we might glean. What we project on our fantasy selves says a lot about reality selves. Adam Davis was an overweight, bullied kid, so the characters he liked to play tend to be dexterous, cool, and suave. Greg asked what conclusions might be drawn about a person who only wants to play a magic user.

"A cry for power in your life," Adam Johns immediately claimed. He didn't even think about it! Just *bam*! You roll a one on Autonomy checks, sad, powerless wizard!

Someone get me a couch.

I immediately rebuffed that observation. That wasn't me at all. But it kept nagging at me. How can I crave power when I feel like I already have too much? I control the Amazon subscriptions that magically fill our shelves with protein powder and saline solution. I control the autopayments so our bills are never delinquent. I administer the flea medication and make sure the rabies vaccinations are up to date for the pets. It is my inbox that gets jammed with 3,862 email messages from my son's school every week. Sounds like what I crave is less power, but that doesn't happen because I am also a bit of a control freak. I crave order and organization to keep the anxiety away. Maybe what I really wanted was to experience chaos and disarray in a

---

1. Shelly: An already filled-out and ready to use D&D character sheet—great for new players!

safe space. Do it in someone else's home! I love wild magic after all.[2] Ah, yes, I need more randomness in my life. Let go of control! Stop monitoring how Bart loads the dishwasher and just let it go! Wow. See how fun and easy that was? I need a drink.

As a parent, my heart broke and repaired itself about 184 times during this interview. It broke thinking about seeing my kid struggle. It mended thinking of these parents putting their trust in a game I work on every day. It broke thinking of these kids longing for social connection. Then it grew three sizes when the Adams confirmed D&D was helping them do just that. This game was something they had in common. They were forming genuine friendships. Many of them continued to play together outside of therapy.

With every session, the Adams did an intro and outro to help kids mentally prepare for what's to come or unwind from what their characters experienced. They talk about what they found challenging and how it was overcome. They took time to acknowledge the success of other party members and compliment their efforts. Overall, the focus remained on being a team player and the social rewards that come with it.

Although there's no age limit on whom Wheelhouse Workshop works with, the majority of their clients are kids.

"Adults," according to the Adams, "are more resistant to the idea of play."

Adults aren't always good at making the best choices when it comes to their health. Plus, it's harder for adults to make friends. It helps if you have an activity to rally around, like happy hour, a sport, or reloading the dishwasher after your husband loaded it. Gaming is the perfect activity for this. Maybe that's why so many of my closest friends are people I met through work.

A really cool part of this interview was when the Adams shared breaking news. They were about a month out from launching their new initiative, Game to Grow. They couldn't tell us much at the time except that Game to Grow was meant to serve an even greater purpose and take the work Wheelhouse Workshop was doing and reach a wider audience. Greg and I have been following the adventures of the Adams and the altruistic empire they're building. Today Game to Grow is thriving and continues to promote applied gaming and reach even more people with a wider scope of challenges. They

---

2. Shelly: Wild magic is untamed magic that can cause a secondary, unplanned, positive or negative magical effect. It is freeing and delightful. Don't let anyone tell you otherwise.

offer training and consultation services to other therapists and gaming advocates around the world.

Greg's mom used to say she knew a lady whose son was into *Dungeons & Dragons* and that's why he didn't have friends. Ironically, it's exactly the reason so many kids do have friends. In addition to this new, fun fact to drop at his next family dinner, Greg said he also has a bevy of characters struggling with "mommy issues."

Better get a bigger couch.

Greg

Deven Rue Creates Magical Map Portals

I'm convinced that maps are magical transportation devices. I watched the animated *The Hobbit* film when I was six years old, and witnessing Elrond making the moon runes appear on the map of the Lonely Mountain was probably the exact moment I began loving fantasy. That moment led to my older brother showing me the map in the opening pages of the book, and I was elated to see it was the same image in the cartoon! When he told me the author himself created that map—well, dear reader, I very much wanted to be J. R. R. Tolkien after that. You know, with a cooler name. Like G. R. E. G. Tito.

That experience led to me spending hours in my room with a pencil, a big pink eraser, and a piece of paper. I would doodle a coastline, draw some mountains and forests, and put some rivers and towns here and there. None of it made a lick of sense as far as weather patterns and plate tectonics, but after a few hours I would have a continent full of storytelling possibilities. I still have some of those physical maps in my game room as I type this, even though I've moved around the country and ended up more than 3,000 miles from my childhood bedroom. My early maps still transport me to another world, another place.

That transportation magic is evident in the work of Deven Rue. She's an artist who specializes in creating maps for some well-known fantasy lands like Taldorei and Exandria from *Critical Role* and D&D's Barovia.[1] Deven now primarily creates maps of not-so-widely-known lands that people commission her to create so they can immortalize their homebrew D&D campaign. I followed her work for years on Twitter before we got the chance to

---

1. Greg: Borovia is the gothic horror setting of the D&D adventure *Curse of Strahd.*

speak in February 2019 to learn about her process and how she started this jaw-dropping career.

Shelly and I often talk to guests who learn something about themselves through the positive experiences they've had while playing D&D. Shelly gobbles these anecdotes up like they were peanut butter M&Ms, especially if the growth experiences occurred when our guests were young. Seriously, these stories get her blood pumping more than a *Bachelorette in Paradise House Hunter* marathon coming on at the gym! The experiences they tell us about usually revolve around something really engaging or happy occurring in the game, such as the swing of that first axe to overcome their feelings of inadequacy. Or maybe crushing on that NPC and discovering their attraction to a particular gender or type.[2] (Elves for me.) Sweet and/or heroic moments, right? That's not exactly how it went down for Deven becoming a cartographer. Deven's love of maps was sparked by her friends at the D&D table getting into a throwdown argument with the DM!

The argument concerned their party's location in the world. Sixteen-year-old Deven was tired of hearing their shrill voices complaining about where the goblin camp was in relation to the town or whatever, so she waded in and drew a quick map to graphically show how wrong the arguers were. The argument quickly moved on to something else, but the DM kept looking at the map Deven jotted down. "That's really good," they said. Deven was buoyed by this comment, and she started to think more about maps.

The next day, she went to her earth sciences teacher and started asking nonstop questions about how the world worked. She learned about mountains and archipelagoes and hills and rivers and lakes and weather patterns dumping water in particular locations to form wetlands or rainforests. Her teacher was psyched because she was very engaged in the material, but Deven used it to inform her newfound love of creating fantastical landscapes on paper.

Deven's skill with the quill leveled up over many years as she continued playing D&D and LARPs through her twenties. Live action roleplaying is like taking the game of D&D, usually played sitting around a table, and putting it on its feet. Instead of merely describing how your character might look, act,

2. Greg: An NPC is a character played by the DM, which can lead to all kinds of exploration since the DM may be presenting as a male and playing a female role or any other variation in between when interacting with players.

or feel, in LARPing you have the chance to act out the swing of every sword with a foam-clad prop while carefully curating your costume so you appear closer to the image of your character inside your head. LARPing is usually played outside with dozens (if not hundreds) of people over a longer period of time than a usual D&D session, like an overnight or a weekend.

"One of the things I love about LARPing is the moment you arrive, you are in character," Deven said. "And you get to stay in character the entire time. It's a really immersive experience."

Immersion is a common theme when talking to Deven. She told us she played five D&D games a week at one point in her life—she didn't just dunk her toes into D&D, she cannonballed whole hog into the hobby. We're talking full immersion, people.

When she couldn't play with her friends around the table or whack each other with foam swords in a field, she would open up a single-player RPG on her PC like *Skyrim*, the *Elder Scrolls* game from 2011 that captured the feeling of having an evocative landscape to explore pretty much however you wanted. *Skyrim* provides a really effective in-game map that just begs to be filled in with secret locations uncovered by the player. But Deven's immersion wasn't complete without a physical map to peruse, and she couldn't help herself from making one herself because she was disappointed with the one that came with the game.

You see, kids, back in my day, you had to go to a real store to actually purchase a physical video game on things called discs; it didn't just beam directly to your GameBox. Some video games, especially of the RPG category, would put physical artifacts in the game box, like a compass, an in-game item like a jewel or a ring, or an actual cloth map. I'm not sure exactly when the practice started, but I remember seeing maps ship with games like the Ultima series in the 1980s. (I still have one of those somewhere.)

The one that came with *Elder Scrolls V: Skyrim* in 2011 just didn't cut it for Deven, and that ended up being the inciting incident that led to her career as a full-time fantasy cartographer. "[The map] didn't look anything like the map that was in the game, and I was like 'I have to fix this,'" she told us. "So I did. And I started posting it [online], and I got a bunch of people who were like 'You can draw maps? Can you draw me a map?'"

"That's actually what the internet first discovered me by," she said. She began to charge folks for making maps. After turning down the inevitable requests for maps of established worlds from fantasy movies or video games—"Copyrights, sorry!"—someone asked her to create a map for their own worlds they explore in D&D. "If I can make one map, I can make another, and it started to snowball from there," Deven said.

Now she doesn't make maps like it's her hobby-job, it's her real-life job-by-job. That's right—her actual career is making maps and selling them online. Shelly asked, "When you were sixteen doodling your first D&D map, did you ever think this is a job? Like I can get paid and make a living doing this?"

"Every kid wishes that when they are playing video games or playing D&D where they say 'Oh man, what if I could do this for a living?'" she said in a very dude-bro voice. "And now *I do this for a living*. Fourteen-year-old me is losing her mind right now."

It's not just maps, though. Saying she only makes maps is a bit of an understatement since Deven has done a really good job in branding and marketing her work. She runs a very successful Patreon, which brings in a steady revenue and shares the load of commissioning maps—which can cost thousands of dollars each—with a larger group of her community. She develops that community through a Discord server and Twitch streams in which she creates some of her maps live on camera while chatting with her viewers. All of that is centralized at her website, where she also sells apparel featuring her maps and other work, prints of maps, map weights,[3] and other accessories.

She's even put her D&D character out into the world for people to use in their games. Deven Rue, the tiefling cartographer, is 20th-level and uses a custom-made ranger subclass she contributed to designing the mechanics for.[4] Deven even worked with a miniature figure manufacturer to create a mini of this character. You can grab it from her website and bring this amazing character to life in your game right now. If that's not putting yourself out there, I don't know what is!

What you wouldn't think of when you see Deven's outstanding visual art skills is that she is visually impaired. Working with props and maps have a profound effect on her because the tactile feeling of those objects is sometimes the best way for her to engage with the story. Being mostly blind in

---

3. Greg: Small, yet heavy little metal items that hold down the corners of the map that may curl up after being rolled for a long time.

4. Greg: You can download this custom-made material Deven worked on with Hannah Rose from the Dungeon Masters Guild, a website where you can upload material using D&D rules and IP like the Forgotten Realms and make some money through sales.

one eye, Deven doesn't have good depth perception. "I live in a 2D world," she told us before saying she didn't really discover how differently she viewed the world until she was in her twenties.

It's something she went into more detail on when she returned to the podcast in 2020 and talked about the D&D game she was running. She said she had teamed up with a Dungeon Master who was hearing impaired, and they ran a game for a group of players with impairments they shared. "We can make it so everyone at the table can understand what's going on."

Deven told us that to make other visually impaired people comfortable at the D&D table, the best thing to do is to talk with them about easing any difficulties they have in how the game is presented and describe things in ways they'll understand. "For most people who are visually impaired, we absolutely love textures and tactile things," she said. "When I go to describe any scene, I explain things in a very tactile way. [I'll describe] something that feels cold and smooth and metallic, and even use those words to describe a mood of a room. Or the look of a player, so my visually impaired players get a better sense of the mood you are trying to build."

That led to Shelly remembering a scene from the movie *Mask* where Eric Stoltz describes colors to his blind girlfriend Laura Dern using physical props like a hot potato for "red" and cotton for "white fluffy clouds." It's no surprise that Deven immediately knew the scene she was referencing and started quoting it better than Shelly was! That's how she suggested getting across the storytelling information of D&D without relying on describing just what the characters see, since some may not have the frame of reference.

Maps are a visual reference, but Deven is quick to point out they are storytelling devices too. They depict a landscape, but they are as much a creation of the mapmaker as a book is a creation of an author. "Maps are a representation; they are not exact. They can't be even if you want them to be," Deven said. That's an important thing to impart, especially to young people who may not realize that maps like the Mercator projection of our planet was used as a way to diminish the importance of landmasses in the Southern Hemisphere over the more powerful, bigger-looking countries in the North. We're all a bit freaked out at Greenland's massive size! I mean, look at it! The Greenlanders are going to take us all over!

That's why it's important for D&D players and Dungeon Masters to use maps as a way to communicate. "A map should tell a story," she said. "It's not just a functional thing to tell people 'There's a road here.' It should really inspire your players to get out there and do something." In other words, to play *Dungeons & Dragons.*

Deven prefers cloth as a medium for her maps. Although she has done it on parchment, paper, and even leather for the map of the Forgotten Realms she made for Ed Greenwood's birthday,[5] she said that cloth provides the best canvas—pun intended—for absorbing the inks and allowing easy transportation. That's why most ancient maps intended to be used in the field were created on cloth to start with, she told us. They could be rolled up easily without damaging the work and brought on a ship or across a desert.

That fact can make the physical maps used in a D&D game a big part of increasing the immersion around the table. It can make players forget they are playing a game for a moment and embody the characters investigating a map just as the players are at the table. Like the map of the Lonely Mountain from *The Hobbit*, it is fascinating when the imagination of a group of humans are in two places at once, anchored by a physical object. The map exists in both worlds; the group of modern-day humans looking at it around a table and their characters, personas they've created, heroes from another world, another timeline, are also looking at the object. A map is truly a magical item.

That's what D&D is all about!

5. Greg: Greenwood is the creator of the Forgotten Realms setting, purchased by TSR back in the day.

On a Fart Quest with Aaron Reynolds

My best trait as a kid was my love of reading. If my mom wanted to distract me from practicing my Miss Piggy karate moves or take a break from watching me perform one-act plays retelling *Mommie Dearest* from Joan Crawford's point of view, she handed me a book. When I had read and reread all of my books, I started on hers, which is how I went from Judy Blume to Jackie Collins in one afternoon.

My love of reading followed me into adulthood. The best thing about 2020 was having more time to read. Without any social plans, travel, or the will to get off the couch, I spent hours on the patio reading every evening after work and all day on weekends. Bart is also an avid reader. So when I was pregnant, we asked friends and family to give Quinn a book to start his library. Clearly our kid would be a reader! What choice did he have?

The thing about kids? They never take the obvious road. (A Dungeon Master's nightmare!) Despite the books overflowing from his bookshelves, Quinn was a struggling reader. It started in kindergarten, where five-year-olds were expected to emerge with the vocabulary and literary skills of a 1970s third-grader. He struggled with sight words and had no interest in reading a page or two on his own from his favorite board books. In first grade our numbers-loving kid struggled in math, because first-grade math is all word problems. There were tutors and specialists and apps. We tried gamifying the learning, incentives for reading books, and dedicating time every day for family reading (scrolling Instagram counts, right?). My son's apathy toward reading broke my heart. Reading was a gift. How could I make him fall in love with my favorite hobby?

Then a global pandemic hit, he was forced into remote learning, and there was a reason I was a theater major, okay? I'm not great at math, especially Common Core math, and as it turns out, teaching wasn't really my strong suit either. What he lacked in reading aptitude, he made up for in theatrics. What can I say, my kid loved an audience. In first grade he earned the Expressionator Award for his lively performances of the Elephant and Piggie books by Mo Willems. This was an amazing confidence boost, and we started to see his interest piqued in reading books out loud. Because teachers are amazing, he made incredible progress, but he still wasn't quite at the expected level. We knew we needed to find books that inspired him.

Then one day I saw a tweet by Cam Kendell, illustrator extraordinaire who worked on *Dungeon Mayhem: Monster Madness*, about a new book series he was working on, Fart Quest by Aaron Reynolds.

Well, my interest was piqued. Not sure if you know this (unless you're a regular *Dragon Talk* listener), but I'm a big fan of one-cheek squeaks and backdoor breeze humor. I come from a long line of potty joke enthusiasts. My proudest parenting moment came when my four-year-old responded to my mom's assumption the foul odor in our living room was emanating from his pants with a very blasé, "The one who smelt it, dealt it, Granny."

A few days later book one in the Fart Quest series arrived. As Quinn was getting ready for bed, I brought it into his room and casually left it on his shelf.

"What's that?" he asked.

"Oh, just a book a friend of mine worked on," I said, oozing nonchalance. "Sounded cool. It's about farts!"

"It looks like it's about D&D," he answered, noting the trio of young spellcasters on the cover.

"Huh," I said. "I guess. Maybe I should read it?"

He agreed, and within seconds we were cracking up. The first line of the book is "My name is Fart." Freakin' brilliant! Then the strangest thing happened. Quinn took the book out of my hands.

"Can I read it?" he asked.

This whole nonchalance thing was getting tougher to maintain.

"Sure. If you want," I said.

Did someone just cast *comprehend languages*? Because my reluctant reader was reading! And he was good! He didn't care if he mispronounced a word or had to ask for help. He even did voices! He was reading an actual middle-grade novel and he was liking it. After he fell asleep, I went online to buy every other book by the author and discovered something I had missed. Quinn was right. This was a very D&D book. Right there in the author's bio it said, "As a longtime Dungeon Master and lover of *Dungeons & Dragons*, Aaron is no stranger to epic quests."

Now I had a quest: I must meet this Aaron Reynolds.

My goal for inviting Aaron on *Dragon Talk* was simple: tell him I love him for getting my kid to read. He was immediately likable and exactly the kind of person you would expect to write children's books about a protagonist named Fart. Quinn, who liked lurking in the background of every interview in hopes one of the Paul brothers would discover him and make his YouTuber dreams come true, was suddenly camera shy and introverted. He managed to issue a very quiet compliment to his new favorite author.

"I like your books," he said and ran back to his room to practice his *Fortnite* dance moves.

The number one rule for farting in our house is to read the room or you risk clearing the room. Know your audience! Clearly Aaron knew what his middle-grade readers wanted, and that was farts and fantasy. While he probably discovered farts much earlier, Aaron's foray into the world of D&D struck when he himself was a middle-grade reader.

It was the summer of 1981. He was at his buddy Andy's house playing Atari when Andy's big brother extended an invitation to play this strange, mysterious fantastical game. Aaron rolled up his first character that afternoon, a human fighter named Griden the Rebel. Andy's brother gave the party a handful of gold pieces and sent them off shopping. Naturally he blew it all on swords. Soon after, Griden the Rebel embarked on his first dungeon crawl (which Aaron later discovered was actually *The Keep on the Borderlands*),[1] and his mind was blown wide open. Here was this game where you invent the story as you went along. You encountered monsters and treasure! You could die! Up to then, his big imagination was something that got him into trouble. Now he realized it had a purpose. D&D made him realize there were stories in his head that needed to be told. That Christmas he got a copy of the

---

1. Greg: One of the most well-known early D&D adventures that stands the test of time pretty well since it has a clear goal but the party is able to go about it however they choose. It was *The Keep on the Borderlands* content that shipped with D&D Next playtest in 2012 for players to get used to the new rules.

Monster Manual, which he still has along with many other original tomes. His writing and storytelling skills really shone a few years later when he took up the mantle of Dungeon Master. He fully believed he would not have become an author if not for D&D's creative boot camp.

The story of how Fart Quest came to be is almost as divinely prophesied. Aaron's editor, Connie, was highly collaborative and creative and hosted a brainstorming session to talk about what his next project should be. The publisher was looking for a new "potty humor" series, and while Aaron loved a good poop joke as much as the next guy, he wasn't sure he could write a whole book laced with fart puns. Later in that meeting, he rolled high on an Insight check as it was discovered Connie was also a D&D player. We knew that as soon as he described her as collaborative and creative! They couldn't believe it had taken this long to discover their shared hobby and started geeking out immediately as kindred adventuring spirits are wont to do. His agent was there like, "Uhhhhh, what madness has been uncovered here? Can we get back to the butt trumpets and barf patties, please?"

Connie had a wishlist of her own and on it was (not surprising for a D&D lover) an old-school epic fantasy adventure book. Aaron suggested combining these ideas and seconds later they both shouted, "Fart quest!" (And I thought our work meetings were fun!)

Fart Quest is the story of Bartok, a misfit, chubby mage apprentice at a hero academy, who earns the unfortunate nickname of Fart after picking *Gas Attack* as the first spell he wanted to learn. During the annual hero wilderness training, his masters were obliterated by goblins, and Fart, along with the much more competent monk Pan Silversnow and Moxie Battleborn, the brainy dwarven warrior, must decide if they should return to school or venture off on their own and get hands-on hero training. Aaron deliberately created Moxie and Pan to be empowering representations of female characters. No sidekicks here. They're dominant, heroic, and knock every adventuring party trope on its head. The unwitting group of heroes from different backgrounds coming together to solve problems and save the world is a familiar story hook for adults, but it's a great reminder for eight-year-old kids who happen to love a good poop euphemism.

There are a lot of poop jokes and booty-burp puns (and I love them all), but Fart Quest has so much more. And a catchy motto: "Behind the fart, there's a whole bunch of heart." There's a whole bunch of nods to D&D icons like a professor named Master Elmore.[2] You'll also find references to *Tomb of Horrors*, *Caves of Chaos*, and other classics.

Aaron was Dungeon Mastering weekly for a group consisting mostly of women, including his once very confused agent. He can't help thinking about what his fifth-grade self would think about his future self. Not only does he still get to play D&D as a grown-up, but he plays with women! He gets paid to write books about magic spells and toilet humor.

What would have happened if Aaron went to a different friend's house that summer day or if the regulars showed up for Andy's brother game? D&D probably would have found its way to Aaron one way or another, but there's no denying something magical happened on that day in 1981. While his imagination went into and stayed in overdrive from then on, Aaron could not have fathomed how forty years later in the summer of 2021, he'd do the same thing for my kid.

2. Greg: Larry Elmore was a prolific fantasy illustrator and painter. You may have seen his paintings on the covers of the first Dragonlance novels.

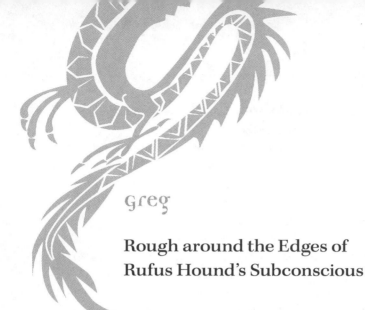

greg

Rough around the Edges of Rufus Hound's Subconscious

I'm a sucker for self-deprecating British comedy. From Monty Python, Mr. Bean, and *A Fish Called Wanda* to *The Office* (UK) and the films of Edgar Wright, there's a long line of sarcastic Brits who don't take themselves too seriously that makes me squirm with delight. Rufus Hound is definitely on that list.

He had a very long and intimate story to tell. It may not be perceptible to everyone listening to our episodes, but some of the interviews on *Dragon Talk* are easier for us than others. Whether it's a guest's unfamiliarity with public speaking or not wanting to hog the spotlight, there are sometimes questions that don't get a lengthy response and we have to scramble to make up a silly joke or throw another question out quickly to keep the conversation going. Internal dialogue: Oh, I thought asking about the passion project you've been working on for forty-seven years was going to garner more than a four-word answer. "Tell me about your pets!" [*screams in interviewer*].

That was not the case with Rufus Hound. His skill and practice in doing Radio 4, appearing on talk shows, and generally being a gregarious actor doing standup comedy or theater meant that he commanded his presence on the *Dragon Talk* "stage" pretty damn well. Especially when you consider that he was calling in at 11 p.m. his time from London.

Rufus's story starts out like my own history with D&D. As a kid, he had the desire to play and had all the books but was never able to find a group to teach him. "I had been trying to play *Dungeons & Dragons* for years," he said. "I bought the books. I bought the kits. I had the starter set I think when I was eleven that I got from Sam Goody. And I had just always found it impossible.

I lack the brain power or just the mindset really to be able to sit with those books and work out how to turn it into a game."

That's something that we often hear from folks. It was hard to parse the mechanics, rules, and guidelines in those early editions of D&D and figure out how to play the game without the experience of someone inviting you to a table to try it out. That's honestly why D&D is taking off so much right now. Listening to podcasts or watching streaming shows of people playing D&D removes that barrier. But poor Rufus didn't have the luxury of Twitch or YouTube or an iPhone back in 199whenever. Before he knew it, other interests grabbed his teenage attention.

"It's something I really wanted to do up until I was about thirteen," he said. "Then there were girls. Then there was drinking. And that lasted me basically until the start of the pandemic."

It wasn't until romcom-like fate stepped in that he was able to live his best D&D life. After an aborted attempt to learn to run D&D from the *Stranger Things Starter Set* for his own teenage boy, he was lucky enough to go to a wedding in late 2019 and be sat next to none other than writer Paul Foxcroft. In the usual get-to-know-you banter at a table of misfits, Paul casually dropped that he played D&D in his lists of interests.

"We're all making polite wedding small talk," Rufus said. "'How did you get here?' 'Yeah, you know a hybrid is a good idea' . . . Then off-handedly Paul just goes 'I run and write D&D sets.' And I was like '*Stop! Wait! Fuh! Ha!* I've been reading the *Stranger Things Starter Set* and I thought I would be able to get the hang of it by now, and I'm a forty-year-old man and I do not know how to do this!'"

I'm sure the other wedding guests just faded into the middle distance while Paul and Rufus talked excitedly about D&D. Paul agreed to DM for Rufus and his son's friends, and they had an amazing six-hour session in which they heroically got through half of the adventure. Rufus got a theater gig that took him away from home for a little bit, and by that time it was March 2020, and we all know what happened then.

In many ways, this is a pandemic story. It can't be overstated how much show business professionals were affected by the inability of audiences to congregate indoors. Rufus called Paul and asked if he could join a regular weekly streaming game of D&D. That was all the rage on the internet, right? Maybe playing D&D could help while Rufus didn't have anything else to do except drink beer. Maybe the pandemic would mean he could finally play in a campaign! When most people play games during the evening, Rufus had always had to be at work doing shows. But with that silly time sink we call "work" removed, he could finally play D&D!

He joined the cast of *Questing Time*, which (full disclosure) was created in collaboration with Wizards of the Coast's UK team to draw in more of a local audience to D&D. The character Paul asked him to run wasn't very different from himself, as you kinda do with your first D&D character to ease yourself into roleplaying. Rufus and Paul called his character the Rough Knight— often shortened to Rough. While Rufus was describing his character as a rough-and-tumble dwarf with a thick Scottish accent and a penchant for drinking lots of beer, I was gleefully unaware of the dramatically heartfelt turn this tale would take. I don't think Rufus really knew either at the time.

Something he was realizing when the pandemic hit, however, was that his marriage wasn't long for this mortal coil. "About six weeks after lockdown started, my wife and I made the decision that we need to call this a day," he said. "We'd known for a long time things weren't great. Because of my job, I was away a lot, and then suddenly I was present all the time. And that shift was more than enough to convince the pair of us that whatever we were, 'husband and wife' should no longer feature on that list." They decided to continue as friends, coparents, and "two people generally invested in not making anyone else's life awful." He moved out, staying with his family only half the week, while the other half he lived in a friend's spare room.

Luckily, Rufus still had D&D to play and beer to drink. As he shared with us his gloriously sculpted beer belly profile,[1] he made sure to make us aware that English people have a strong penchant for drinking. Culturally. It's what they are good at! Combined with a metric fuck-ton of marriage-ending, pandemic-fueled free time, Rufus admitted he drank even more than usual.

In the D&D world created by Paul Foxcroft on *Questing Time*, Rufus found some escape. By this time, fans had flocked to the comedy stylings of his first ongoing D&D campaign, and he was surprised and delighted by receiving fan art of his character or the strange thrill you get when doing something for a lark that ends up being meaningful to a whole bunch of people. The story

---

1. Greg: Rufus described his beer belly as the most expensive thing he owns. It's heavily curated with fat cells created from various alcohols he's consumed throughout his career.

goes on for a few months, and Rufus said he derailed the campaign Paul had planned by putting a *bag of holding* over a portal and sending everyone in the party to a whole other plane of existence.[2]

In the bizarre, magical, crossroads city called Sigil,[3] City of Doors, the party decided to get tattoos. You know, like every other sailor in port, except because this is D&D, the tattoos would all have magical effects. Clever DM Paul added a special bit in that the characters don't get to decide what is tattooed on them in this particular shop. The magic chooses what tattoo goes on your body, which the party was game for since they know it will be interesting or at least entertaining. Most of the tattoos ended up being pretty comedic. For example, one gave the character the ability to turn into a goose at will, which sounds funny on its own but was actually in reference to previous moments in the campaign. "If you've watched hours and hours of us playing D&D, it made perfect, hilarious sense," Rufus said.

Then it was Rough's turn. The Rough Knight sat in the chair for his tattoo, and he asked how much it would cost. "Your pain and regret," came the reply. Apparently the 300 gp Rough had prepared wasn't going to be enough. The tattoo artist then said, "How much?" As in, how much of his pain and regret would he like to pay?

This took Rufus aback. His surly, drunken dwarf character stepped away for a moment to think it over while another of his mates got inked up. Then he came back to sit in the chair. "How much?" the artist asked again, needle in hand.

"All of it," said Rough.

At this point, all his mates went nuts IRL, as the kids say. They were screaming and yelling in surprise at this decision. The Twitch chat went nuts too,[4] and even Paul tried to make sure Rufus knew what a momentous deci-

---

2. Greg: In D&D a *bag of holding* is a portable extradimensional space where characters can store way more than they could carry because anything that goes in the bag actually goes to another dimension. Characters can grab stuff out of it safely, and maybe even climb in to hide if you hold your breath, but the downside is a *bag of holding* interacts with other portals to other dimensions in, shall we say, interesting ways. Don't even think about putting a *bag of holding* into a *portable hole*.

3. Greg: Detailed in the *Planescape* setting.

4. Greg: When broadcasting on Twitch, viewers can chat together, and that's sometimes visible to those playing. It's a substitute for crowd interactions that I'm sure Rufus was missing. It's one the greatest ways the platform provides a sense of community, for better or worse.

sion this is. "They are all going 'No no no no! Think this through. What's that going to change? You're going to end up with a character now who's totally different. If you let all that go, then who is this guy?'" said Rufus.

He didn't really hear any of that. He had been approaching this character like any role he would play in a theater. After taking the moment to think on it, the decision to give up all that pain and all that regret was something he believed the Rough Knight would absolutely do. "As an actor, you get the script [and you ask] 'Who are they? How does their mind work? What is true for them?' and then you just play what is true." If you swap "script" for "character sheet," that sounds like a description of how D&D can work. "It never crossed my mind at any point that the Rough Knight, being given the chance to absent himself of all of this pain and regret, wouldn't take it."

So he did. In the game, Rough closed his eyes, and when he woke there was a large warhammer tattooed on his chest. This was no ordinary hammer. It was a depiction of a famous magic weapon called Whelm that, to Rufus's understanding after he researched D&D lore for a few days, carried the weight of pain and regret of being stolen and used by a vampire to murder its dwarven creators.[5] (This is D&D after all.)

Rufus was inspired to write a poem about all he's learned and how the Rough Knight has changed and perhaps recite the poem at the next session. He very quickly wrote the "Ode of Whelm." It is all about Rough attempting to relate to his compatriots exactly how transformative this experience was for him.

"To lose your pain and to lose your regret, is to accept that who you were yesterday doesn't need to be who you are today, and it doesn't need to be who you are tomorrow. Nobody asked to be born. You get what you are given. You make the best of it. If that's not good enough, and if you have regrets, that's okay. But then you set about changing them. You set about atoning for them." Those lines would fit pretty well as a daily mantra for most of us, right?

After he got the verses written, he realized it would probably work better as a song. He got in touch with a musician friend of his, John Smith,[6] and sent him the lyrics. John was about to start his next album, but he said if he had

5. Greg: Whelm is a magical weapon that first appeared in a seminal adventure from the 1980s called *White Plume Mountain*.

6. Greg: "One of England's premier singer-songwriters" with a "voice like buttered diamonds," according to Rufus. Check him out at https://www.johnsmithjohnsmith .com/.

time, he would give a go at putting some chords to the "Ode of Whelm." Rufus fully expected to get nothing back from him, but then a couple of days later he receives a fully produced MP3 with guitar, strings, and vocals all backing the lyrics he had written. You can listen to it on YouTube now.

> The hammer that you hold
> With flame and anvil made
> Is neither tool nor weapon at the start
> Whether to be bold
> To love or be afraid
> Is decided as the bellows goad
> the forge inside your heart.

"When I listened to the song played back to me," he said while fighting back a sob with a forced laugh. "I realized I had written a song to warn myself to get help."

This is how D&D changed Rufus Hound's life.

Rufus acknowledged the strangeness of writing a poem from the point of view of a fictional character about a fictional hammer to explain to other fictional characters what was going on in the fictional character's psyche. "I had created enough steps of removal, of emotional distance, that I could write that none of us asked to be here," Rufus said, full on crying at this point in the interview. "It's okay if life hasn't turned out the way you want it to turn out. Some of it will be your fault. But now, what do you do from here? What do you do to make it better? How do you accept the situation and then move forward to make things better? Which is what I needed to hear. I needed to hear, 'Get help.' It took this many layers of removal for my subconscious to shout at me."

All of that came flooding to him after listening to this song. A few very important tumblers fell into place so that it all clicked. His name is Rufus Hound. He'd been playing a D&D character for six months called the Rough Knight, often shortened to Rough. He didn't know until that moment that he had created an avatar by which to process all of the pain and upheaval he had been feeling in the cursed year of Pelor, 2020. His job as a performer disappeared, his sense of purpose vanished, and his role as a parent had shifted with the breakup of his marriage. He was living in a friend's furnished shed, so his sense of place was shattered too. Everything was fucked. And that was okay.

"Within a couple of weeks, I had stopped drinking," he said. "I started therapy. All whilst still playing D&D."

"And the changes that occurred for Rough started to be the changes that were occurring for me, Rufus."

D&D changed his life. For the better, I might add. Creating a situation where you, as a character, can talk to yourself, the real human, in a way you couldn't before, to get across important ideas, is just one of the wonders of this game. Over the years on *Dragon Talk*, we've heard that sentiment from a lot of people, but none quite as entertainingly as Rufus Hound told it. I laughed a lot during this interview. I cried along with him. Ups and downs. Comedy and tragedy. Games. Life.

shelly

Gary Astleford: Man with a Badge

I joined a Brownies Girl Scout troop when I was seven years old. It was not what I expected.

By then I had already tried and flamed out mightily with ceramics, gymnastics, swimming, and tap dance, so no one should have been surprised by my short-lived stint with the Girl Scouts. I was not a joiner. I was a snap-judging dabbler.

Yet my mom spent money on a uniform that consisted of a brown vest, starchy short-sleeve white button-down shirt, and a pair of bulbous khakis. I loved the color brown, but in small doses. I went to three meetings and realized these nature-loving do-gooders were not for me. They didn't even sell cookies! I'm pretty sure my mom was livid—at me of course, but also at herself for financing another of my frivolous flights of fancies. In the end, I abandoned my troop and haven't worn khakis since.

I might have stuck around longer if my troop did fun stuff like form an adventuring party to banish evil spirits from a town or return a baby owlbear to her parents. How cool would it have been to earn a first aid badge by crushing it as a cleric? Maybe slap a "Fair Play" badge on that brown vest as a reward for my collaborative and cooperative storytelling. But that sounds improbable. Kids—especially young women—don't get rewarded for playing games. Certainly not back in my day. Most parents wouldn't be pinning demon-slayer badges to their daughter's sashes.

I feel for kids these days: social media, early puberty, remote learning basically eliminating the concept of snow days. But they also have Alexa to explain what a reflexive pronoun is, on-demand entertainment, and now the ability to earn bad-ass badges for playing D&D thanks to writer and designer Gary Astleford. Our first interaction was over email when Gary sent a message asking if I would help with the tabletop roleplaying game workshop he was putting together for his local Girl Scout troop in Southern California.

Wait, what? A roleplaying game workshop? For Girl Scouts? Uhh, could I still fit into those bulbous khakis?

I completely fell in love with Gary's idea and was eager to help, including asking him to be our guest on *Dragon Talk* to help spread the good word of Dungeon Scouts, the website he put together to share resources on how to bring the joy of roleplaying games to Girl Scouts.

Gary's history with D&D dated back to grade school and the magical visiting oasis of book fairs. Remember those glorious days when your school's gymnasium was transformed from the place Matthew Benny almost knocked the braces off your teeth with a kickball to a literary paradise? Folding tables piled with the latest treasures from Beverly Cleary, Paula Danziger, and Judy Blume. I must have been too smitten with *Garfield in Paradise* to notice *Dungeon of Dread*, but Gary was immediately drawn to the Endless Quest books. From there, it was a quick jaunt to the *Monster Manual*, which he discovered at a local bookstore and purchased with money he begged from his parents. More than thirty years later, he still has that original *Monster Manual*, which must make his parents feel pretty good about their investment.

The idea for the Girl Scout badge workshop originated after he saw the short documentary *D&D&G* by Meredith Jacobson. The film follows a group of girls totally unfamiliar with D&D as they are introduced to the game and a group of boys who play it weekly. Because of his daughter's involvement with Girl Scouts, Gary spent a lot of time with girls around the same age as the girls in the documentary and he loved the idea of going against gender stereotypes. In addition, he fully understood the positive effect that roleplaying games can have on a young person's life. This was his way to pay it forward.

The workshop was open to girls ranging from fourth to ninth grade. How does one earn a badge for roleplaying (because I'm still waiting for mine)? Gary knew it was important to give the girls a primer on what roleplaying games were before dipping into the basics like classes and races, abilities, and what's with these weird dice. They created their own characters and prepared for adventure in Elustra, the homebrew world Gary crafted specifically for this workshop. I would spend about fifteen minutes on Pinterest looking for Bundt cake recipes to bring to my kid's workshop. Gary brought an entire universe.

Adventure can take many forms, especially for new players. Gary didn't care if the girls played D&D by the book, made up their own rules, or even made up their own game entirely. He wanted the focus to be on their characters and collaborative storytelling. As a way to accelerate the immersion, Gary grounded the fantasy with a bit of reality by incorporating familiar elements into the story, like parts of the Girl Scouts mythology. Elustra was ruled by Queen Sunblade, who formed a group called the Queen's Knights. Once inducted into the order, one must swear by the queen's law, which was basically the Girl Scout Promise with a few in-world changes. As the girls recited the Queen's Knights vows in character, they recognized its real-life origins and understood the significance of their fantasy-world post. Each girl was asked to choose a line from the vow that her character would adopt. Would they be courageous and strong? Would they vow to make the world a better place? It was reminiscent of the bonds and flaws system in fifth-edition D&D and was such a cool, simple way to make players feel invested in their characters and the story (while also tying it directly to the Girl Scout mantras). I wanted to give Gary a badge for all the effort he put into this event!

We talk a lot about the moment when a new player "gets it." It's almost like you can see the lightbulb go on above their head. "Wait . . . I can do anything? Like whatever I want? And the dice will tell me if I succeed?" It's an amazing sight to behold. Gary saw it happen many times during the workshop. The girls started off shy and reserved but warmed up to roleplaying by interacting with NPCs. They were given horses, which of course they loved. (Except one girl who had her heart set on a unicorn. She was told there wasn't one in the stable that day, but she should come back another time.) They were creative problem solvers, using animal handling to calm, rather than kill, a wolf that was hunting them. (It worked!) They dove into combat when it was called for and stood up for their fellow members. When you're used to games that are competitive, D&D was a pretty special reprieve.

Upon completion of the workshop, the girls got what they came for: a beautiful patch with an embroidered dragon and a d20 designed by Gary himself. They also got a copy of the basic rules and their own dice set. Perhaps the biggest takeaway was the connection with their peers, confidence from trying and succeeding at something new, and the possibility of meeting a unicorn if their timing was just right. Gary encouraged the girls to keep playing, maybe start a club at their school or library, keep teaching others, and if they feel the spark, become a Dungeon Master. Obviously, they will, and for that we need a DM badge. Thankfully Gary was already working on that.

Now, thanks to Gary, there are teen girls in SoCal begging money out of their parents to buy their first *Monster Manual*. Think of that next time you're asked to buy a box of Thin Mints.

Greg

Pretending to Be Evil When
You Are as Good as Lauren Urban

I n many ways, the interview with Lauren Urban in 2016 was a
turning point for the podcast that was eventually called *Dragon
Talk*. When we talked to her in a small conference room at the
Wizards' offices in March 2016, we were still calling our show "the *Dungeons & Dragons* podcast." She lived near the offices in Renton, and came to
hang out with us in person, which was a real change of pace. At that time, the
D&D marketing team was actively talking about ways to ramp up Wizards'
support of programming in the greater community. Lauren, also known as
OboeCrazy, was a big part of that process early on, and I'll always associate
her ascension in the community as a bellwether for what would come. She's
a lightning rod of positivity, which is why it was odd to go back to this interview and listen to her describe running a D&D story from an evil character's
point of view.

When we met Lauren, she was a professional oboist who made her bread
and butter by playing in orchestras and ensembles in the Seattle area. She got
into D&D a few years back, and eventually turned her friendly pop-culture
podcast into a weekly D&D session called *Dungeons & Dragons & Drunks*—
shortened to *Dungeon Drunks*, now called *Distinguished Adventurers*—that's
been running for hundreds of episodes since 2017. She's gone on to work at
various companies, including Wizards, as an advocate for the community.
Such an astounding amount of happy coincidence and wonderful success
surrounds Lauren that you start to realize it's really because of her that all
these people around her are so happy.

Lauren's kindness is a living, breathing thing.[1] Lauren was a fixture in the Wizards office and never failed to say something insightful or inspire those around her when she came to visit. She once gave me an unexpected Hanukkah gift of a pair of fuzzy green striped socks that I still cherish. Sometimes a hug from Lauren was the only bright spot of the day, and I treasured it each time. Compassion like that is on display whenever she talks about her D&D players too. When Lauren is the Dungeon Master, everyone feels like they are getting one of those cherished hugs while playing D&D.

That's why it is so strange to hear her recount what it was like to run an evil D&D campaign. It's important to note that roleplaying as a "evil" character doesn't necessarily mean that everyone pretends to be Snidely Whiplash twirling a mustache and tying damsels to the railroad tracks or psychopathic serial killer stuff. The storytelling is just going to be a lot grittier in an evil campaign. Playing as an evil character generally feels like embodying the antiheroes you might recognize from popular media such as *Deadpool*, *Breaking Bad*, *Dexter*, or *Conan the Barbarian*. Players and the DM agree that they aren't doing the normal hero crap of saving kittens or leaving witnesses alive. It's an agreement that this campaign ain't gonna be a feel-good coming-of-age type of storytelling. Distilling D&D to the basic ingredients of killing monsters and taking their stuff and focusing on that type of selfish gameplay can be super fun. Usually, playing an evil campaign or session is a palate-cleanser before getting back to the heroic fantasy the game does so well. Usually.

How did Lauren end up running an evil campaign for nine months? She had been playing with the same group for years, and they switched campaigns and DMs fairly often. Someone would run one and burn out, or another would end in a TPK, a Total Party Kill, when every character in the group dies in the middle of a fight and there's no one there to revive them. The way Lauren ran D&D, that's when you hung that story up to dry and started working on something else.

"It was a random thing that I said in the middle of one game," Lauren said when she made a joke about running an evil campaign. "And everyone was like, can we do that?" So they tried it out. Many of the tenets of D&D still worked, and that's because Lauren used some really simple storytelling truths.

---

1. Shelly: No truer words. Lauren is one of those people who celebrates the success and happiness of others. She's the most genuine person I know. We're all better off because of Lauren.

"I always feel like the best villains don't view themselves as villains. They think they're the hero in their own story," she said. "It was just a matter of giving them an adventure where they could reconcile in their heads that 'I'm saving the world. I'm doing the right thing by getting this artifact that's going to let my goddess take over the world and slaughter anybody in her path. That totally makes sense!'"

Oddly enough, that campaign didn't end in a TPK. "Evil people won. Darkness now enshrouds the land," Lauren said in a deadpan voice. "It came to a happy? Sad? Happy? It came to an end. And my players were happy." That's all that matters. That's what I mean about Lauren. She's always working hard so that those around her are not just comfortable but having fun being the weirdoes they are.

I think Lauren might be the only *Dragon Talk* guest who has actually run a D&D campaign for me as a player. When I played with her during Clerical Error in 2018, we wanted to try something different. I asked Lauren if she wanted to DM a campaign concentrating on the low-stakes storytelling taking place among a found family group in the city of Waterdeep. She jumped at the thought of running a comedic campaign—Clerical Error is D&D mashed up with workplace sit-coms like *Cheers* or *Parks and Recreation*.

She made sure everyone's storytelling desires were realized. For example, I wanted to play as a blind character. I had been talking to advocates in the D&D community about increasing the representation of disabled characters in play.[2] I asked Lauren if the cleric I was making for this show could be blind, and she immediately brightened up at the notion and worked with me on how to make it happen seamlessly in game. When the time came for Faben's tragic backstory to be told in a drunkenly comedic way, she was happy to give me the spotlight. Of course, I've had many years of experience "acting" intoxicated to fall back on.

Lauren supports everyone around her, whether it's allowing experiments in edgy storytelling or working with me to showcase disabled characters in a D&D game. To this day, she watches so many of the streaming D&D campaigns of the many friends she's made in this community that I often wonder if she isn't some kind of magical time traveler. Aspiring DMs and people can learn a lot from her, including how to run an evil campaign without losing faith in her players' goodness or humanity in general.

---

2. Greg: Shoutout to Jennifer Kretchmer and Blind Temple for inspiring us and providing guidelines for playing a disabled character.

Giancarlo Volpe, a Dragon Prince among Men

My friend and neighbor Kari has three imaginative, active, outdoorsy children. (On my side of the fence, daylight makes it hard for my child to see his iPad screen, so he's seldom seen outside.) Her kids provide the soundtrack to our neighborhood with their made-up, old-school play where they could take a couple of rocks, rope, and a pile of dirt and create a game keeping them entertained all summer. Usually, I could tell what games they were up to by the way they talked to each other: Popcorn on the Trampoline, Pirate Ship Unicorn Invaders, Fairy Dream House Makeover (my favorite). One afternoon I heard unfamiliar sounds coming from their direction. Something about "bending air" and turning on the hose, even the occasional "I'm telling mom if you use real fire!" What the heck was going on there?

Later that week I walked by Benji, the youngest, while walking our dog.

"Hey, Benji!" I called out.

"I'm not Benji," he replied with authority. "I'm Aang!"

"Oh, okay," I said, figuring Aang was five-year-old slang for "angry." No need to get too deep in that. I'm sure Kari had it all under control.

That evening I heard Benji's sisters referring to him as Aang. Jeesh, one bad mood and you're saddled with a nickname for life! But then I heard him call one of his sisters "Sokka." Then a huge fight broke out over who's turn it was to be the Avatar. My son looked up from his iPad and rolled his eyes. Sometimes I loved having an only child.

I asked Kari what was up with the nicknames and attempts to light the neighborhood on fire.

"Oh," she laughed. "It's that show on Netflix called *Avatar: The Last Airbender*. They're obsessed. All of them."

Apparently, they've watched the whole series multiple times, and when they're not watching it, they are outside trying to bend the elements to their will. (Let's hope Benji never fully comes into his powers.) Serendipitously, a few months later we booked one of the directors for *Avatar*, Giancarlo Volpe, for an interview.

Giancarlo and his lovely wife, Angela Marie, came to our offices for the interview. When you're chatting about someone's love of D&D you kind of forget they're a big deal, award-winning Hollywood director. He had an Emmy! Stars are just like us when it comes to D&D! Sometimes your character stops an assassination attempt on a Lord of Waterdeep. Sometimes you roll a one and hit yourself in the face with your own arrow.

Giancarlo is a well-known producer, animator, and director for critically acclaimed TV shows like *Star Wars: The Clone Wars*, *King of the Hill*, *The Dragon Prince*, and of course *Avatar: The Last Airbender*. He admitted almost everyone who works in animation plays D&D or has some history with it. He was currently playing *Out of the Abyss* with a group of mostly animators. Of course, they illustrate their characters, and throughout the game they doodle key moments as they're happening.[1] At the end of the night, you can see everyone's interpretation of that fiery battle with a hook horror.[2] He was playing a monk in that campaign and enjoying his time as a player but missing the creative freedom of Dungeon Mastering. He reminisced about when he was DMing for the *King of the Hill* crew back when they were all single, employed, and had discretionary free time. Giancarlo would craft his own dungeons out of papier-mâché.

Greg and I are obsessed with writers' rooms and jumped at the chance to ask an industry expert all of our burning questions about them. Fortunately, Giancarlo didn't burst our bubble too much and explained things in a language we understood. Showrunners, the people responsible for maintaining the creative control of a TV show, were essentially the Dungeon Masters.

1. Shelly: Follow Giancarlo on Instagram at @giancarlo_volpe to see some of his drawings.

2. Shelly: A hook horror is a two-legged humanoid creature with a vulture-esque head and hooks for hands. Just your run-of-the-mill bad guy.

This person, instead of the dice, was the arbitrator of decisions. The writers were the players. While the showrunner/DM guides the overall narrative, the writers/players fill in the details. Working with a showrunner who has mastered the art of collaboration, thinking on their feet, and wrangling a table full of creative thinkers must be a huge bonus.

One of Giancarlo's most memorable turns as a Dungeon Master also lent itself to a great writers' room trick. He was teaching a group of new players and was trying to keep the rules behind the scenes so as not to overwhelm them. Instead of telling them what needed to happen next, he simply asked, "What would you do now?" Never mind what they *could* do. As they came to their decisions, he revealed the rule pertaining to that action. If a player wanted to kick down a door, he explained how to roll a Strength check. If they wanted to spend some time looking around, he asked for a Perception or Investigation check. Some of his players were avid video gamers who slowly discovered they were no longer on rails. It's that moment we always talk about! You can see the creative circuit board in their brains light up. He sometimes used this same tactic in the writers' room to discover (TV) character motivation.

There's a lot of parallels between writing for a TV show and DMing. My sticky-notes-on-the-wall fantasy wasn't completely far off. When planning a season of television, say, thirteen episodes, the showrunner creates a square for each episode. Writers fill in the different squares with a rough idea of what will happen in each episode. You know where the main characters start and where you want them to end, and the team fills in the stops along the way. They create dilemmas, challenges, conflicts, other characters throughout, keeping the story momentum going until the last episode where everything climaxes, and the main character's demon (literally or figuratively) is confronted. Do they succeed or fail, confront or succumb?

What happens in episode three can dramatically affect what happens in later episodes, so only a few episodes are written at a time. Now that we live in a time of on-demand, instant gratification entertainment that we can consume in marathon sessions, every episode needs to end with some element of suspense. Kind of like weekly game sessions. It's a bit more prescriptive than leaving it up the dice, but still a cool tip for campaign planning.

Giancarlo's approach to writing TV for children was also good advice for anyone who has younger players at the table. Treat them as you would anyone else. Leave out gratuitous or suggestive stuff, but don't talk down to them. They'll pick up on that in a minute and trust me, it won't end well. We also noted how kids tended to watch shows over and over again, which made them more discerning viewers, so don't even think about cutting corners. You can and should have flawed, troubled characters, but create them in a more "ethically conscious" way. (Maybe save Walter White from *Breaking Bad* for your adult friend game.)

My son and Greg's daughter (who act like they are the same brain split in half and are each other's greatest audience) love horror and scaring each other. Their favorite game is pretending Pennywise, the child-murdering, sewer-dwelling clown from Stephen King's *It*, is in the house threatening to make them his next victim. It freaks me out but is fun for them. Giancarlo told us about one of his own childhood fears, and I still think he should somehow turn this into his next series. As a kid, he was terrified of the band KISS. Seeing them in their black and white grease-painted goodness was absolutely paralyzing. "Ahhhhhh, why is his tongue so long?!" Totally fair question, young Giancarlo. He believed KISS lived in his garage and whenever he needed to go in there, he'd sing "Popeye the Sailor Man" to keep Gene Simmons's tongue at bay.

With such a long history with D&D, it's no wonder you can see its influence on Giancarlo's work. He brings a little piece of D&D to all his projects, but perhaps *The Dragon Prince* felt like the biggest nod. The premise of the show centers around a war between humans and elves. The elves have dragons and magic on their side, which to me sounds like the most unbalanced fight since the Avengers versus Thanos. The humans discovered a dragon egg, and the only chance for peace depends on three children delivering it safely to the Dragon Queen. I love this story premise for a bunch of reasons, but especially because it shows how kids can use their wits, instead of violence, to be heroic.

I was hugely inspired by the premise for *The Dragon Prince*, and not only did Quinn and I watch the entire first season in a matter of days, I found myself taking notes on running a campaign inspired by the story. D&D inspired Giancarlo, who inspired me, who will hopefully inspire the kids I want to introduce to the fantastical world of *Dungeons & Dragons*. The quest is one giant circle.

Greg

Making It Rainn Wilson

I t's not often that you get to speak to someone who played a huge part in the cultural history of the twenty-first century. The US version of *The Office* was the biggest show on TV when it was broadcast for nine seasons on NBC from 2005 to 2013, and the character of Dwight Schrute is memorable as being the quirky foil to Jim Halpert's charming lead. Dwight is still a key figure in memes and internet culture today as marathon watching on streaming services has kept *The Office* ever present in our minds. What may not be clear until you read about his interview on *Dragon Talk*, though, is that actor Rainn Wilson used one of his old D&D buddies as an inspiration for his character.

That's right people! *Dungeons & Dragons* inspired *The Office*. (At least indirectly.)

Shelly and I had a few things going for us when we booked Rainn for an interview in late 2015. *The Office* was off the air by that point, and Rainn had taken the time off to pen a memoir. The press tour for that book, *The Bassoon King*, led him to taking our request for an interview. The book mentions growing up in the Pacific Northwest—not too far from where I'm currently typing these words—and playing D&D back in the late 1970s/early 1980s, so there was a bit of a connection. But I really think we got to talk to him mostly on a lark.

Book tours are grueling endeavors. I've never been on one myself (that is, until Shelly and I come to your local bookstore to promote this tome), but I've talked with enough authors to understand that the schedule can be brutal. You want to maximize your time on the road, so a two-week book tour can mean ten to twelve appearances at stores with a plane or bus ride overnight between each stop and phone interviews or radio appearances during any spare hour. It can be the Nine Hells for authors, especially if they aren't used to such a rock star schedule. Let's face it, many authors are more comfortable with a mug of tea and a comfy couch at home than having a microphone and screaming fans in their face.

I think Rainn agreed to an interview with the official D&D podcast in 2015 because he thought it would be a nice deviation from the norm.[1] It's something he could tell people as a funny anecdote. "I even spoke to the nerds at Wizards of the Coast for this book, can you believe that?" He mentions in the opening moments of the interview that he thought talking to us would be "funny." Not fun, or heartwarming or engaging. Funny. That's us!

We only had thirty minutes to talk with him, but I'm still thankful for the opportunity since there are so many great nuggets in the interview. My favorite part of it was just how ingrained he was in the gaming/fantasy/sci-fi scene back then.

Rainn told us his father wrote a "crappy" fantasy novel named *Tentacles of Dawn*, so he was always going to conventions with him. Keep in mind that 1981 was way before sci-fi or gaming conventions were big business. Gen Con was still in Wisconsin, PAX wouldn't debut in the Seattle region for more than twenty-five years, and San Diego Comic-Con was only drawing a few thousand attendees after starting nine years earlier. For Rainn to go to a convention like Norwescon in the SeaTac Hyatt was a pretty niche activity. Add to the fact that he played D&D there and was awarded second place in a character contest and you could very much believe he was a gamer through and through. "I came in second place, I really should have won it." The cosplay competition wasn't as intense back then, I guess.

He was a fan and even submitted a monster stat block to TSR back when they published D&D in the 1980s! He describes his monster idea as an Air Leech, and they would do damage as a flying swarm. The publishers of *Dragon* magazine wrote him back—this was before the internet, so this was all done through snail-mail correspondence—and complimented him on the idea even as they rejected his submission. Which was rare, he said. He was very proud of that rejection letter!

"Do you know how TSR douched me over?" Rainn asked us next, referring to the company that used to publish D&D back in the 1980s. A few months later, *Dragon* printed a monster that was very similar to Rainn's idea, something like "Oxygen Vipers" that also flew around in swarms. Shelly and I are

---

1. Greg: This was before we renamed it *Dragon Talk*.

still trying to get to the bottom of this story. The offer stands for us to print his original Air Leech stat block in a D&D publication. Just send it in again, man. We promise not to rename it this time.

To start the interview, Rainn read an excerpt from *The Bassoon King* detailing a schedule for weekend gaming when he was a kid, and it sounds pretty much like *Stranger Things*, *Red Dawn*, and *The Goonies* all mashed together. Making fun of his teenaged friend's Adam's apple—"It's like a baby alien was stuck in his pale, freckled esophagus, threatening to break out at any moment"—banging on each other with broomstick swords, wielding garbage can lid shields, and defeating the *Dungeons of Aktar* while scarfing pizza are all worthy endeavors for a teenager into D&D in 1979.

I asked Rainn if he kept up with any of his friends from those days. We had heard from so many older fans that the bonds forged around the table sometimes last for life. He demurred at first, and I realize now it's probably a little hard for an actor to admit they haven't kept up relationships with past friends. He mentioned he had a few brief conversations with those folks in the years since, but nothing too substantial. That's when he made an entreaty to us to perhaps reconnect with one of the friends with whom he played a lot of D&D and with whom he'd lost touch: Chris Cole.

Chris was the friend who had a real bow and arrow and loved doing target practice by throwing knives at tires. Rainn said he used his memories of Chris to inform his portrayal of Dwight Schrute. The plethora of weapons stashed in the office of Dunder Mifflin, the slavish devotion to shows like *Battlestar Galactica*, and the odd obsession with peak male performance.[2] According to Rainn, the skinny Chris had glasses that had the logo of the Lorne Greene *Battlestar Galactica* emblazoned on them, and he only played "muscly barbarians" in D&D. Even Chris's eventual path of joining the army as a cornet player seems extremely "Dwight-like" to me.

Sadly, Rainn hasn't heard from Chris since then. Presumably, even after our entreaties during the interview to help track him down, he has yet to reveal himself. So this is one last ditch effort. Chris Cole, if you are out there reading this, give Rainn Wilson a ring. He wants to thank you for your participation in D&D youth rituals that informed one of the greatest roles in modern American television. You deserve at least second place in a character contest at Norwescon.

2. Shelly: Wasn't he also obsessed with bears and beets?

Decades and Dragons with
Robert Wardhaugh and Jason Hashimoto

've been in many D&D games with the best of intentions. We shall play every Monday! We will level up to 20! We shall never split this party! Like young, dewy-eyed lovers, we thought our campaign would outlast all others. We were meant to be. We were so well-rounded. We even had a cleric! Then someone went on maternity leave and work got busy. Someone got a new job, and someone (gasp!) quit the group! We fell apart. I thought I'd never find another D&D group to love me like they did. Until I did.

My longest group lasted for two years, which I thought was a tremendous run until I heard about a history professor from Ontario, Canada, named Robert Wardhaugh who had been running the same game of *Dungeons & Dragons* for nearly forty years. *Forty years!*

When we interviewed Robert for the first time in 2016, his game was only in its thirty-fourth year, so really, not that impressive. We were so in awe that we invited him back for an update eighteen months later and spoiler: the game was still going strong. Since then Robert's game, known as The Game, has caught the attention of larger media outlets like CNN, the CBC, and even *Popular Mechanics*. It likely is the longest continuously running game of D&D ever.

We interviewed Robert along with Jason Hashimoto, one of the players in his campaign. Jason brought the story to Greg's attention. He had seen people play D&D and was intrigued by it, but Jason hadn't tried it himself until he met Robert. Seeing his extensive collection of miniatures and terrain bringing to life the world he had created,[1] was more than enough to inspire

---

1. Shelly: Robert's collection of miniatures has more than 20,000 items!

Jason to jump in. Robert could basically create any environment imaginable and, coupled with his dazzling storytelling skills, that is what draws in new players and keeps his existing players coming back decade after decade.

That was ten years ago, and Jason hasn't stopped playing since.[2]

Robert was fourteen in 1982 when it all began. He grew up in a small town of about 250 people in western Canada. When a visiting friend came with the *Advanced Dungeons & Dragons Starter Set* and some rulebooks, they taught Robert to play. His life changed forever. Nearly four decades later, he hasn't stopped playing and changing other people's lives because of it. He was totally hooked, much to the dismay of the mostly fundamentalist community he grew up in. What attracted him was how the rules could be pushed and manipulated, unlike the board games he was used to. It was almost like D&D was alive, constantly changing and bending at the will of your imagination.

His friend returned home and took his D&D books, with the exception of the *Dungeon Master's Guide*. Robert got his hands on a *Monster Manual*, but knowing the rules were "just a guide," he felt confident he had more than enough to get started. Even without the *Player's Handbook*, he was able to see how the rules were designed and filled in holes where needed. Between common sense and what his friend told him, he was creating his own system. He tested things out by DMing for one other player, and after he gained some confidence, he expanded to five players. In a town of 250, that's a pretty sizable party! Robert played all through high school, then college, and grad school, and with every stop, he met more people who played or wanted to play D&D, many of whom he still plays with today.[3] The game has continued with sessions one or two times a week, consecutively, for nearly forty years with the longest breaks only being a few weeks due to things like weddings, honeymoons, and babies.

The world Robert created is brilliant and inspired by his love of the past. Leaning into common sense again, he realized there was no need to invent a whole new world when there were plenty of great ones found within the pages of his history books. His world is an altered version of our historical world blended with other popular gaming and fantasy concepts. You can visit Middle-earth. South America has been replaced with the entire world of

---

2. Shelly: He's also the party photographer, and you can get a peek at their game table on Instagram at @thegamednd.

3. Shelly: One of his players has been in the game since 1985.

Robert E. Howard's Hyboria. Dune exists in the deep deserts of Arabia. This world has literally been decades in the making.

Want in on this game? It's not totally unreasonable. Robert loves introducing new players to the group and watching their characters develop. You only get to see that fresh perspective once, and it has generational appeal. Some of the new players are children of his longtime players. It all comes full circle. Currently Robert has about fifty players! He probably wouldn't notice a few more, right? Not everyone attends in person because Robert's connections span the globe. He has players dropping in from all over the world, and it's seldom the same group twice. The characters are all different levels too, which I love because I always felt like it was unrealistic that an adventuring party all had the same experience. Chances are, when you meet in a tavern or find each other tearing off the same phone number on an Adventurers Wanted poster, you would have wildly different skills and training. I love the idea of my 3rd-level wizard cowering behind a 13th-level barbarian. Sometimes I need a little reality with my fantasy.

Now you might be wondering how Robert manages all of these different players coming in and out of the game in his world and around the table. He has a perfectly logical response for that. They are all members of the same mercenary group, and the pendants they wear allow them to teleport between worlds. "Worlds" in this case is Robert's game world and a kid's soccer tournament. I love the idea of showing up to the game in real life and having no idea who you'll be adventuring beside that day.

Of course, having so many players means many different player types and personalities—a significant challenge for a DM with only a handful of players. How does one Dungeon Master keep everyone happy?

"The story," Robert said, and Jason agreed.

With a tale so expansive and detailed, there will always be something to appease every type. For the most part, they all get along, but if not, that's okay too. Robert allows real-life squabbles to be played out in the game. Who knows? You might end up with a cool backstory or plot hook that way.

I wondered what it was like to play a character for so long. I get attached the second I give them a name, so after a decade or two they would pretty much be family. Be careful in Robert's game, because if your character dies, that's it—no *resurrection* spell for you. Deceased characters get a nice funeral and plenty of time to refill their drink and peruse Robert's minis looking for inspiration for their next character. It sounds harsh, but as Robert explained, the reality is, death has to mean something. No do-overs! You don't get a "Oh well, I've been itching to play a monk anyway" moment and then hit up the character builder for a redo. Robert believes that fearing your character's demise is the best way to create a sense of reality. While this terrified me to no end, I got it: decisions informed by a healthy fear of death matter. If I were a Dungeon Master committed to four decades of the same campaign, I'd want my players to feel invested too. Heck, I was invested in The Game after forty minutes.

To prove Robert isn't a power-crazed DM who plasters his walls with shredded character sheets, we got to the core of why he was so dedicated to this game and the people who play it.

"Friendships are important," he explained. "One of the biggest things this game offers is a way to keep your friends. As we get older, things get in the way and friendships are hard to maintain—especially for guys."

Robert wanted to create something so awesome, so legendary, so uniquely ownable to him, no matter where he was or what was happening in the world, that his friends would still want to come and play. Like a good Dungeon Master, Robert knows how to bring the emotion.

We asked how much longer he planned to keep The Game going.

"As long as I'm alive and able to keep it going," Robert answered.

I'm not sure how, but I have a feeling that even if the former weren't true, he'd still find a way to come and play.

Ending Friendships and Forming
Power Couples with ND Stevenson

Let's be honest. *She-Ra and the Princesses of Power* is a D&D cartoon without any of the branding. The fantasy and gaming tropes on display in the Netflix production are pretty obvious to fans of the game, but I don't think Shelly and I realized just how much the bones of D&D are present in the series. Take the character of Glimmer, for example. Creator ND Stevenson came on *Dragon Talk* in May 2020 and told us that Glimmer was straight up based on the D&D character they used in the first campaign they played with their soon-to-be wife, Molly Ostertag.[1]

Note: Because this episode was recorded after the fifth season of *She-Ra* aired, we got into some spoiler territory. You have been warned.

ND can't really pull apart D&D and *She-Ra* into two separate things. "In my head, they are very woven together," they said. "I started playing D&D about when I started on *She-Ra*. A lot of my experiences from D&D went into *She-Ra*," they added. There's this episode in season one where Adora and her friends are in Entrapta's castle, and ND told us how it was directly inspired by a D&D session Molly ran in which their party was exploring a mansion that was inhabited by automatons. Luckily, ND got Molly's permission before they brought that idea to the writers on the show.

The character ND played in that session was an angsty tiefling warlock who made a deal with a devil just to piss off their moms.[2] "As soon as I unlocked

1. Greg: Stevenson had a different first name at the time of the interview on *Dragon Talk*, and we made every effort to keep the naming consistent with their wishes.

2. Greg: Part of the deal with the warlock class is that a character makes a pact

misty step,[3] it was a nightmare for Molly," they said. "If any conceivable situation arose in which I could use *misty step*, I would use it." They told an elaborate example where, instead of going with their party to the front door, their warlock teleported into the top floor of an arboretum full of anthropomorphic plant monsters, barely surviving the fall, and then running for their life.

"Meanwhile, my teammates just went up to the door, found it to be unlocked. They were welcomed in, there was a feast, they all got new clothes, while I'm sprinting through this indoor forest being chased by plant monsters," ND said, laughing. "I drew a lot of inspiration from that for Glimmer's teleporting. You can get yourself into more trouble than you can get yourself out of sometimes."

Many fans across the sexuality and gender spectrum were joyful at seeing Adora and Catra's relationship mature into something much different than a friendship by the end of season five. Lesbian relationships have long been portrayed negatively in media, or if it is positive, the couple is grown up into adults. It's been extremely gratifying for many in the D&D community to see a teenage relationship mature over the course of a series the way it did in *She-Ra*.

ND was quick to point out how that type of story just isn't seen in media, especially in media for kids. "What happens when you don't know how to define your relationship to [a] person? When it turns out what you thought was friendship was a little more?" ND asked.

ND and Molly are the first official power couple to be interviewed independently on *Dragon Talk* for their own amazing projects. I remember being impressed with Molly's stories of LARPing and running D&D campaigns for their then-girlfriend, and Molly's work on The Witch Boy graphic novel series continues to inspire me and my daughters. Molly has even contributed material to D&D books such as *Van Richten's Guide to Ravenloft*. The Couple

---

with a more powerful supernatural entity to use magic. Modern D&D players love it because it sets up wonderful storylines and built-in relationship dynamics that can be explored by a good DM. Want to do that uber powerful thing? Well, you have to do this quest for the Ancient One.

3. Greg: A common 2nd-level spell that lets characters teleport short distances. It's super useful to, say, blink yourself thirty feet away and flank an enemy or get to the other side of a dangerous chasm.

of Power married in 2019 and, being an unabashed fan of their work, I was happy to see social media photos of their wedding ceremony involving lots of replica swords and badass women posing with them. Thirsty sword lesbians, indeed.

"I like it," ND said when Shelly and I made them blush by complimenting their badassery. "I like being a power couple." While ND was already working on *She-Ra* when they first met five years ago, they definitely wouldn't have integrated so much D&D in the show if it wasn't for Molly. Molly had just moved to L.A. and had started up a D&D campaign to make new friends. "I wanted to be friends with her, and I also wanted to date her," ND said, pointedly. They rolled high on that Persuasion check, I'd say.

The fan response to the first season of *She-Ra* was incomparable, but what's interesting is that their writing team had already written five seasons before they received any feedback from fans. "Our writers rolled off before season one even aired," ND said. So there was no way to adapt the story based on any response, but the one thing it did was convince them that they were on the right track. The arc for those two characters was always meant to be about heartbreak and, after many misadventures and shenanigans, a possible reconciliation and affirmation that their friendship had matured into a romantic relationship.

"When it comes to Adora and Catra, I had made a gamble that they were going to be a ship, a pairing, a relationship people would be invested in." It's a little bit like rolling the dice, isn't it? Will the audience like what I've made? You need to get a fifteen or higher on your Persuasion roll.

But it worked! The show rolled a nat twenty! "People did latch on to Adora and Catra," ND said in 2020 after the final season had been shown on Netflix. "I feel really lucky, and I feel really glad that they saw what we were trying to do and are so passionate about it. . . . The response to season five has just blown me away."

What's exciting about *She-Ra* is that different moments or characters appealed to so many different types of people. Not only were my daughters fans of *She-Ra*, but Shelly told an adorable story of how her son got into it, especially digging Glimmer's teenage sassiness to her mother, the queen. "He loved Glimmer," Shelly said. "He spent the rest of the night going, 'Mom! God! You never let me do anything!'"

An experience we've all had but rarely talk about much is how friendships change and evolve over time. I cycled through a bunch of different friends when I was growing up, and it always hurt when I lost any closeness with them. Look, Mike, I'm sorry I accidentally pulled the shower head out of the wall of your parent's bathroom, and I had to get out uncleaned and tell you there was water streaming inside the drywall. Getting a severe poison ivy reaction all over my leg after we played in the woods behind your house during that sleepover was technically *your* fault. Is that why we never hung out outside of school again?

The portrayal of that type of thing in *She-Ra* was important to my family. My oldest daughter, Edna, had a rough time in school with one particular friend. We'll call the friend Wendy, and Edna adored her so much in first grade. Wendy could make her laugh more than anyone else her own age. Wendy held court in the cafeteria with a few other girls, bestowing them all with her hilarious performances mimicking one of the teachers or saying things that are only funny to six-year-old girls. I can attest to there being a lot of giggling. Like, *a lot*.

At some point, Wendy stopped including Edna in her circle. She would only let Edna back in if certain conditions were met, such as running to get Wendy's lunch box for her. Edna would do it but would also feel upset that this person she thought of as a friend would take advantage of her like that. Wendy would also loudly make fun of Edna's love of pets and get the rest of the circle laughing at her. My poor daughter had a lot of nights crying with us thinking about this girl and wondering why she didn't like her all of a sudden. Edna thought there was something wrong with her, and we had to assure her she was awesome, and that Wendy just maybe wasn't a good enough person for her to hang out with anymore. A six-year-old isn't really well equipped to deal with that knowledge.

That's why it was important for Edna to watch the first season of *She-Ra* at that age. The relationship between Adora and Catra was clearly not the same situation—as far as I know, my daughter is not a trainee in a pseudo-fascistic police state, nor a princess of power—but I think the hurt that those characters feel about their relationship changing meant a lot to Edna. A lot of her school life had focused on Wendy, and that ending badly was a big deal to her young psyche. A friendship ending like that is not really a part of growing up that's seen in a lot of programming or literature out there for kids.

"I don't see it a lot, even in media that is about friendship—like [we see] how 'Friendship is the most important thing,' which I agree with—but I've never seen a story like this in children's media that is like, 'What happens when you lose a friend? What happens when you lose someone who is the most important to you in the entire world?'" ND said. "Stories like that would have made a world of difference to me at that age. The first time I lost a friend—I still think it hurts more than any breakup I've ever had. It's something I needed to show and get into."

In between choking back tears on the mic, I thanked ND for portraying that relationship so well and how meaningful it was for Edna. I get so emotional when I'm talking about my kids growing up. (Of course, I also cry at car commercials and basically any movie or musical, but that's a whole other story.)

By exploring the relationship between Adora and Catra and how it evolved over time, ND made a choice to focus on the characters' internal struggles. It's important for people to see themselves in the media, and *She-Ra* did that extremely well without making it code for bad or evil, as it is so often shown in cartoons or animation from previous decades. I appreciated, and I think others did too, how their relationship resonated for all people, regardless of gender or maturity. It's the embodiment of "show, don't tell" that is an important mantra for good storytellers everywhere.

That's also true of how much D&D tropes are wrapped up in the show. It wasn't just traipsing out magic swords, mystical archers, and warriors of destiny, though. The whole idea of how these characters were formed in ND's production was derived from the player dynamics. In my humble opinion, ND did a better job at bringing that to life in a children's animated show than many films and novels that have attempted the same.

"I felt like the experience of D&D was so wrapped up in my conception of the characters and the world, and how we were interacting with the world," ND said. "Just like when you are playing D&D these characters have decided what roles they are going to play, and they are trying to fit those roles. But sometimes they roll really badly and they don't do a great job of fitting into those roles all the time."

I pointed out how ND deftly used "roll" and "role" there.

"Yeah, I know," they laughed. "You gotta keep up. It's word play. That's why they pay me the big bucks."

That word play is worth a dragon's hoard of gold!

Alicia Marie: A Wonder of a Woman

Have you ever met someone incredibly gorgeous, funny, talented, creative, strong, and fit and liked them anyway? Me neither! Until we met Alicia Marie. What sorcery is this?!

Alicia is a costume designer, creator, author, accessibility advocate, and fitness guru who was our guest in spring 2021. We were finally coming out of the darkness of 2020, full of hope and new beginnings! Things were just starting to open up again. We were vaxxed, waxed, and looking forward to seeing the noses and mouths of our favorite people once again. In a way, Alicia embodied all of this as she was no stranger to hope and new beginnings.

When Alicia popped up on our computer screens, she was sitting in front of what looked like the workroom from *Project Runway*. Commissioned costumes in various stages of completion, bolts of fabric, half-dressed mannequins that (not gonna lie) freaked me out a bit. How do you just live with those things? Hasn't she ever played *Betrayal at House on the Hill*? She admitted the mannequins do tend to freak people out, but she enjoys their company.

I'm not a cosplayer because there is not a crafty bone in my body and I have bad memories from terrible homemade costumes of my youth, but I often find myself wondering how my characters would be outfitted. How did they dress for a day in town shopping for supplies versus heading into the remote wilds for an adventure? I love the idea of each character wearing some item of significance like their beloved grandmother's robe or a coveted ring purchased with money earned from their first successful mission or the face of their mortal enemy skinned and taken in battle. In any case, clothing and accessories aren't just to look good—they're great jumping-off points for backstories.

Alicia used wardrobe choices as a means for storytelling and shared a couple examples from her characters. One was a young halfling sorcerer who didn't have her draconic bloodline wings yet but desperately wanted them. So she created and wore fake wings. One day her brother left without warning, never to be heard from again, so she wore one of his oversized tunics as a way to keep him close. She also had bunny slippers, because why not?

The second example was a mind-reading monk with a mysterious, hard-to-place accent she played at Gary Con. When her character wanted to "see," Alicia closed her eyes and held up her hand, revealing one glassy doll eye glued to her palm. She had a whole jar of those doll eyes just sitting around! (That alone is great inspiration for a character's backstory or some Alicia Marie fan fic, which I was pretty sure I'd start writing after this interview.)

One might think that someone who loves cosplay, fantasy, and art would naturally find their way to D&D, but like a lot of people, the time between Alicia's desire to play and when she finally took the plunge spanned years. Obviously there were lots of crossovers in the cosplay community and D&D, so finding a seat at a table wasn't the problem. Alicia thought she *couldn't* play and was holding herself back, not without reason.

Before her cochlear implant surgery, Alicia was considered profoundly deaf, having only about 5 percent word recognition and 20 percent hearing in both ears. She learned to read lips, and without it, voices were basically "Charlie Brown's parents." Playing a game that involves a lot of talking and made-up words would be angst-ridden for anyone in that situation. She talked about "dinner party anxiety," a common emotional struggle for many people with hearing difficulties, where you know you're not keeping up with the conversation and fear being asked to join in. When you admit you can't hear what was being said, the asker feels awful and uncomfortable because they made you uncomfortable, and then everyone's uncomfortable and it's extremely stressful. Even though her friends insisted they would make it work for her, she rebuffed their invitations to play and followed from afar.

In September 2019, Alicia got a cochlear implant in her right ear. The implant is essentially a minuscule computer surgically implanted on the side of the head. At first, she could hear beeps and squeaks and high-pitched sounds, but after about two weeks her brain started figuring out what words were. Four months later, she played in her first D&D game! This was absolutely fascinating to Greg and me. Now with implants in both ears, Alicia can do things like talk on the phone and play D&D online without anxiety or headphones.

Even though she studied neuroscience in college, this technology amazed her. She works as an advocate for the nonprofit organization No Limits, which provides deaf children and their families the skills needed to be successful in life and school. Science is amazing, y'all.

Alicia's first game of D&D:

- ◆ was with Deborah Ann Woll,
- ◆ was streamed live, and
- ◆ featured 11th-level characters.

Most of us start at 1st level, maybe 3rd if you're an experienced gamer. But 11th?! And live-streamed? Alicia is the kind of person who throws herself into everything. She studied for months and crafted an oversized character sheet made out of poster board and sticky notes to use as a "cheat sheet" during the game.

Alicia was rocking a high Strength score. She could crush the tires of a monster truck in one perfectly manicured hand without even rolling Advantage. Her foray into fitness began when she was eight years old. As a kid, Alicia was "full of anxiety" and, being the only person of color in her school, never felt like she fit in. One day while visiting her older cousin, she discovered a stash of comic books under his bed. She had never seen comics in her life, let alone female superheroes like Wonder Woman and She-Hulk. She loved how strong these women were and how they were drawn. Before this, her only representation of the female body was Barbie and, no offense to the iconic doll, but what's the point of having your arms perpetually bent and ninety degrees if there are no ripped biceps poking out? Alicia realized she could shape her own physique to look like the women in comics. Her mission began. At nine, her mom bought her a set of hand weights and as Alicia excitedly pumped two pounds in each hand, she envisioned her transformation. At ten, she was on her way with tiny defined arm muscles and abs, which was so confusing to the kids and adults in her life. Was she supposed to look like that? Was something wrong with her? Perhaps she should switch to organic dairy? She spent her school lunches arm wrestling (and beating) the boys. Other kids were put off and most likely confused, and they couldn't understand why she'd want to make herself "look like a man."

"I don't want to look like a man," she corrected them and pointed to a picture of Wonder Woman. "I want to look like *her*."

Her fitness journey continued throughout high school and college, where she taught aerobics and eventually started competing professionally in physique competitions.[1]

In 2010 she attended her first Comic Con and cosplayed as Storm from the X-Men. Her costume was so well received, she became inspired to bring all her favorite characters to life.[2] With D&D, she gravitated toward strong, Amazonian, hammer-swinging giantesses because that's her comfort zone, but the more experienced she gets, the more she branches out. There's something fantastical about playing a gnome or a halfling when you're already strong in real life.

I see Alicia's name pop up all the time on social media, and not just because of her amazing cosplay. She's guesting on lots of D&D streams and even made an appearance at D&D Celebration 2021. I couldn't be happier seeing her finally be a part of the community she shied away from for so long.

1. Shelly: Physique competitions tend to focus on aesthetics, proportion, and fitness as opposed to the maximum muscle definition of bodybuilder competitions.

2. Shelly: Follow @aliciamariebody on Instagram to see her looks.

shelly

Creating Community with Dan Harmon

ot take: the *Dungeons & Dragons* episodes on the TV show *Community* were some of the best depictions of D&D ever. They're better than my very best home D&D games—even the one when Hagatha, my hexblood sorcerer, grossed out the party by pulling off her fingernails and yanking out her teeth to use as *magic tokens*.[1]

It helps to have comedy geniuses like Yvette Nicole Brown, Danny Pudi, and Chevy Chase say lines written by a group of creative geniuses, but those episodes had something special—actor, writer, director, producer, and creator of *Community*, Dan Harmon. Shockingly, *Dragon Talk* had him too, which stands as one of the most surreal experiences in my podcast history.

Through the laughs and zingy one-liners *Community* was known for, Dan managed to get to the heart of this game and convey something I've been struggling to put into words for over a decade: the lasting effect it has on the people who play it and why it's still relevant nearly fifty years after its creation.

There were two episodes of *Community* featuring D&D. The first was called "Advanced *Dungeons & Dragons*," which aired in 2011 (season 2, episode 14) and centered around the character of Neil, an ostracized student. Neil was what one might consider the stereotypical D&D player back in the day. He was an outsider with low self-esteem who used D&D to pretend to be

1. Shelly: Gross your party out too with *magic token*, an action hexbloods can take allowing them to harmlessly pull out a fingernail, tooth, or lock of hair; give it to another creature and use it to send telepathic messages to each other.

someone else. Upon realizing Neil was in a dark place, the usually smug and self-centered Jeff (played by Joel McHale) brought the study group together for a game of D&D. Everyone was invited except Pierce, the spoiled, out-of-touch man baby played by Chevy Chase.

Abed (played by Danny Pudi) was the Dungeon Master, and while the uninitiated group bumbled along, their interest was piqued after Neil's character slayed a bunch of goblins with his sword. Everything was going great until a petulant Pierce, angry about being excluded, showed up and demanded to play. Abed quickly created a new character named Pierce, who proceeded to cheat, steal, and split the party, before polymorphing Neil's character into an overweight human. Pierce IRL obtained a copy of the adventure and discovered a powerful amulet. A truly evolved being with a heightened sense of compassion and the pleasure of interviewing therapists on a podcast they co-host might think if someone was that angry and destructive, perhaps they're the one in need of healing. Despite being mocked and shunned for years, Neil could see that Pierce was hurting. Instead of turning the party against him, Neil displayed a remarkable show of empathy. This naturally infuriated Pierce. However, as soon as the opportunity presented itself, Neil's hero managed to destroy the amulet, making the character of Pierce vulnerable once again. Pierce ended up being eaten by a dragon—a most fitting fate. Dan said he thought this was Chevy Chase's best performance of the series, possibly of his career.

The second episode, "Advanced Advanced *Dungeons & Dragons,*" aired in 2014 (season 5, episode 10), a week after our interview with Dan. What made both of these episodes incredibly accurate wasn't just the props, rules, and lore. It was Dan's intimate history with the game. He understood the appeal of bringing seemingly very different people together and the lasting bond of an afternoon of adventure. It was essentially the crux of the show.

This interview was done before Greg came to Wizards. Bart, a giant *Community* fan, was my very eager cohost. Due to Dan's limited availability and our daycare's hours, we had to leave work early, pick up a babysitter, and head home to record the episode in our basement. The first surprise of the interview was when Dan actually showed up! Not because he was a jerk or unreliable but because he was *Dan Harmon*, and he was taking time out of his day to talk to a nerdy, sleep-deprived married couple who were paying a nineteen-year-old girl one dollar a minute to watch a sleeping baby. The second surprise was when he said it was an honor to be on *Dragon Talk*, which might be the nicest thing anyone's ever said to me.

Immediately I outed Bart as a *Community* uber-fan. I wanted Dan to know we weren't some highly paid spokespeople-for-hire who got notes thirty seconds before an interview and had no idea who their subject was.

I made some dumb joke about Bart and me being married, and Dan laughed. Then he was like, "Wait, what? For real? That's adorable!" So naturally Bart and I proceeded to talk all about our dragon-topped wedding cake, how we met at Wizards, and our newborn who was thankfully being quiet upstairs, and oh my God, this was so embarrassing. Was this the Bart and Shelly romance rewind or a D&D podcast? We're pretty sure he was aware we were not highly paid spokespeople.

Bart got us back on track by dropping some fan insights. He theorized that the iconic community college study group was really the model of a D&D party. They were an unlikely band of misfits, each playing a role, who came together to defeat obstacles and solve problems, and developed a strong bond despite their best efforts not to. In every episode, the characters were sitting in the same spot around the same table. Dan agreed. For him it was wish fulfillment to see these characters play this beloved game he discovered when he was twelve.

"There was this kid named Craig who was fifteen and had a skateboard and cigarettes. He was like an alien," Dan recounted.

One day Craig invited everyone over to play D&D in his basement. Dan remembered his brain "just opening up." He was tripping on creativity, imagination, and complete and utter inspiration overload. The other kids were enjoying it, but not as much as Dan was. The things happening in the game were more vivid than what was happening in his real life. Motivated by the desire to purchase Craig's D&D books, Dan started mowing lawns to earn money. He would sit at his kitchen table, reading rulebooks and modules, his brain popping like hot Jiffy Pop kernels through tin foil and realizing how rich and immersive fiction could be. How can you be with real people in a real basement, drinking orange soda and eating pizza, while also risking your life to save a town to earn enough gold pieces to buy that full-plate armor you had your eye on? That's the concept of "bleed" again, when your in-game mood affects your out-of-game life.

So much of *Community* played on themes of imagination and reality and which is healthier or more real. Dan's two planes of existence inevitably collided. After seeing D&D portrayed on shows like *The IT Crowd* and *Freaks and Geeks*, he felt something was missing. In those depictions, playing D&D was the joke and sometimes not even a thoughtful one. Almost any time a character's nerdiness had to be explained, out came the oddly shaped dice and books with fiery, horned devil cover models. D&D was low-hanging fruit for a gimmick, but it could have been so much more.

Dan wanted to tell both stories—the story that happens *in* the game and the story *about* the game. D&D from top to bottom. It was never a question of if D&D was worth playing. It was about what happens when you play. It's articulating the exact moment Dan had in Craig's basement. It's a beautiful thing to behold in real life with people around a table. It's the sign of true genius to see it accurately portrayed with characters portrayed by actors.

Here's the wild part. No one on the *Community* writing staff played D&D or had experience with it. Dan brought in milk crates stuffed with first edition hardcover AD&D books, old dungeon drawings, and character sheets. The inside cover of his *Dungeon Master's Guide* had a blotch of melted wax put there by young Dan because he thought it made the book look cool and authentic. He left this little pile of treasure in the writers' room and took off for the edit bay. It was like the god Thoth cast *legend lore* on the group. Somehow it sunk in. Somehow, they got it.

For the most part, these episodes were incredibly well received by fans, critics, and D&D players, which seems like a 20th-level quest fulfilled. I remember my nonplaying friends asking if that's what D&D was really like, because if so, why didn't I tell them how much fun it was? (I literally wrote two books about how much fun it is, but okay.) But the episodes weren't perfect. The "Advanced Advanced *Dungeons & Dragons*" episode was called out because Chang (played by Ken Jeong), a notoriously antagonistic and unhinged character, showed up to play a drow in a white wig and makeup resembling blackface (later, this episode was removed from Netflix and Hulu because of the blackface). The drow, or dark elves, are a subterranean race of elves created by Gary Gygax, typically portrayed as "bad guys." Shirley (played by Yvette Nicole Brown) is Black and referred to his "cosplay" as a hate crime. Chang defended his actions by explaining that's how the drow looked, which was true, but didn't alleviate her discomfort or the collective cringe from the viewing audience. Chang's D&D character ended up meeting a timely demise, which I'd like to believe was a metaphor for ending that part of D&D's past.

However not everyone involved found any of the subject matter endearing.

The network execs claimed if the first D&D episode was turned in earlier, they would have tossed it in the trash and demanded the team start over. But alas, time was of the essence, so they had no choice but to shoot it.

"D&D pushed their buttons," Dan told us.

The execs thought it was self-indulgent and associated with specificity and inaccessibility. Yet Dan managed to portray a very specific thing being accessible to everyone. The ratings must have changed the execs' minds somewhat because they greenlit the second D&D–inspired episode.

The week after the interview, "Advanced Advanced *Dungeons & Dragons*" aired to a second round of acclaim and more friends berating me for not inviting them to play D&D. I give up. Fine, they can play.

While *Dragon Talk* does a good job shining a spotlight on the brilliant, creative forces in our circle, we've got nothing on Dan Harmon when it comes to building community.

B. Dave Walters Started from the Bottom, Now He's Here

Fighter/mage/thief was a tempting character template back in the early days of D&D. Being able to do basically anything super well in *Dungeons & Dragons* can really do wonders for the power fantasy some fans have. A fighter/mage/thief can fight effectively in close combat with axes and swords, wear armor to protect themselves from stabby things, do impressive amounts of damage if they attack from the shadows,[1] and bend the physical rules of reality with teleportation or solve problems in creative ways with *grease* or *fog cloud* spells.[2] When reality-bending isn't enough, they can convince a guard to let them pass with the help of a *charm* spell or sneak into a vault to unlock it with cunning skill, or they can just blast it all to smithereens with spells like *fireball*. A leveled-up fighter/mage/thief is the D&D equivalent to Superman.

The trade-off was that it takes a super long time for a fighter/mage/thief to become that effective. During this era of D&D, characters leveled or grew in power at different rates, with the basic rule of thumb being the more powerful the character could be, the longer it took to become that powerful. Because the game was built around greater difficulty and characters died all the time, the chances of a fighter/mage/thief surviving until their full potential

1. Greg: The sneak attack is the signature ability of the rogue or thief as it was called to attack unexpectedly, to cause way more damage. Think of a literal back stabbing when the target has no idea the attacker was even there.

2. Greg: *Grease* creates a slippery surface monsters (and adventurers) can slip on; *fog cloud* conjures an opaque puff of fog that can be used to hide a getaway or stage an ambush.

was realized happened about as often as an alien baby crash landing in middle America.

B. Dave Walters is the fighter/mage/thief of the D&D community. When we first met Dave in March 2018, he had already led a whole life as a marketing exec, husband, and parent, and he was a motivational speaker, all while steadily leveling up his storytelling skills through roleplaying. He had done some hosting work at the Geek & Sundry channel on shows like *Ask a Black Geek Friend* and played in live-action games on G&S like *We're Alive: Frontier with Ivan Van Norman*. He had yet to debut as Victor Temple on *L.A. by Night*'s *Vampire: The Masquerade*, or take the stage of *Waterdeep* during the Stream of Many Eyes show I produced in May 2018.

By his own admission, that's when Dave's career really took off, not unlike that fighter/mage/thief finally picking the safe's lock after smashing the burly guard with a mace while casting *invisibility* on himself. Dave took time to develop a series of related skills and has become a superhero for the D&D community, vowing to do good. Mostly.

Let's get back to what it was like before he became so powerful. Dave started playing D&D in Little Rock, Arkansas, when the second edition of D&D was in print in the 1990s. When we asked him what class he gravitated toward, he sheepishly said, "You may recall me saying I was a min-maxer."

"Min-maxer" describes a type of D&D player who would find loopholes or advantageous situations in the rules to exploit to render their characters extremely powerful. Because the math required to play that version of D&D was a bit more robust than it is now, it took folks who could master that math to find these loopholes. Usually. But it also means that the end state is the important part for min-maxers. They are willing to endure many sessions of D&D in which they were throwing nothing but hot garbage at bad guys before unlocking their full potential.

Dave was one of those players. "I was the fighter/mage/thief. I was largely useless for big chunks of the story until it all clicked," he said. For him, the fun of playing D&D was visualizing the endgame for his character and then seeing the story through to get to the point in which his character could achieve that success. Taking a few levels in wizard to dabble in spellcasting wasn't enough; he needed to know his character could have access to the most powerful 9th-level spells in the game like *wish* or *miracle*.[3]

---

3. Greg: These spells are perhaps the most similar to playing make-believe as a kid. They can change the world, reverse time, or bring beloved characters back to life.

"I'm strange, though," Dave said. "I actually hate the leveling process. I hate the leveling process in any game I play. I like the endgame. I like that you are fighting gods and demons and [elder] dragons."

Dave's fascination with the extremely high stakes of the endgame is a theme in his storytelling career. When we were talking about this on the podcast, I posited a D&D streaming show that contrasted characters at the start of their career with their fully formed 20th-level selves. I didn't know it then, but Dave was formulating a similar concept that eventually turned into the D&D–branded comic book series A Darkened Wish, which he co-created with Tess Fowler for IDW Publishing in 2020. In that series, the storytelling flips back and forth between the trials of young, fresh-faced characters meeting up and bashing goblins together and their older, more experienced selves taking on world-ending monstrosities.

Not knowing where a character could end up was something he struggled with. Dave recounted his experience playing in the first season of *Inkwell Society*,[4] in which a group of 0-level characters go through the story unaware of what they are going to be good at in the future. "It is *very* different to what I'm accustomed to," he admitted. "I'm the guy that when the campaign starts, I have mapped my character trajectory from one to twenty. I already know at 4th level I'm taking this feat,[5] at 9th level I'm going to have this ability. I'm *that* dude, so to just show up and have it be 'See what happens' I'm like *GASP*, 'okay.'"

I think Dave had that uncomfortable feeling because of the min-maxing he does in his real life. He might not have known he was going to be a D&D luminary when he was a fresh-faced guy out of college, but there is an element of self-actualization in his persona. He believes he will be successful in his creative endeavors because he sees the 20th-level version of Dave, and he's been working hard to get there! Leveling be damned.

Now it's all coming to fruition. Dave spent decades becoming the man "who says words about things," but it all came together relatively quickly. Shelly and I met Dave in 2018 in our first interview on *Dragon Talk*. After that, I invited him to appear in the live-action off-the-table sessions in *Waterdeep*

---

4. Greg: A streaming D&D show set in the world of Eberron.

5. Greg: Feats, introduced in third edition and carried through to fifth, are abilities you can choose for your character that unlock interesting bonuses or maneuvers like grappling better, altering up your spellcasting through metamagic, or just denoting your character was a good cook a la Samwise Gamgee.

during the Stream of Many Eyes. For many D&D fans, that was their first introduction to Dave as a performer.

Since that moment, Dave has accomplished so much that it almost feels unfair. He runs D&D streamed games and guests on things almost every day of the week, some with fans privately sponsored through Patreon, some public like his horror-themed show on D&D's YouTube channel, *Black Dice Society*. Dave also collaborated with Tanya DePass and other Black creators on *Into the Motherlands*, a crowdfunded Afro-futuristic sci-fi RPG. He has continued to appear on *L.A. by Night* as the vampire Victor Temple,[6] and guested on countless podcasts and conventions and charity events. All this is done while maintaining a healthy dialogue with fans on social media through memes and seemingly nonstop video updates. Dave was even a host of D&D Live 2021, presented by G4TV on a national scale.

All those years of leveling slowly are paying off! This fighter/mage/thief is getting to level 20!

What's fantastic through all of this massive success is that each time Shelly and I speak with him on *Dragon Talk*—he's been on three times now and counting—is that Dave somehow manages to tell me something I needed to hear right when I needed it most. He has brought me to the verge of grateful tears on air several times with his kindness and heartfelt gratitude for what Shelly and I do. In April 2020, about two months after everything started to shut down from COVID-19, Dave came on the podcast and lifted us up.

I said something to the tune of "there's not much we as D&D podcast hosts can do to help make a vaccine" and that playing D&D can be helpful in tricking your brain into thinking you had accomplished something for the greater good. "It is true the real heroes are in hospitals and labs right now," Dave said. "But I would submit that what you guys are doing with *Dragon Talk*, with the [D&D] content,[7] with putting everything out there, is to the greater good. Giving people something to look forward to is to the greater good. You guys, right now, are literally providing a vital human service."

Dave cited Maslow's hierarchy of needs and how, after the physiological

6. Greg: *L.A. by Night* uses the roleplaying game *Vampire* as its basis, but otherwise it's similar to the popular streaming games using D&D.

7. Greg: The D&D team at Wizards of the Coast responded to the pandemic by releasing tons of content for free on the Stay at Home, Play at Home hub on the official website. We wanted to be there for people and encourage them to take up safe activities during quarantine.

needs of food, water, and shelter, there are the psychological needs of belonging to a community that *Dragon Talk* can fulfill for some people. "Being able to just tune in and feel like they are hanging out with you guys, to have a slice of normalcy in the midst of all of this insanity, is huge and significant," he said. "You have contributed to the spread of a lot of joy in this world. And being someone who's been on the receiving end of it, I very much thank you both for everything that you do."

Dave's words buoyed me in a time when I felt I didn't really have a lot of purchase. We were in uncharted territory in spring 2020. Some of us were treading water, doing the things we had done before, only slightly differently because that was our job. What Dave told us on our own podcast—that what we were doing had demonstrable worth beyond the silly jokes Shelly and I make—well, it stuck with me.

I am not a religious person. I've said before on the podcast that I'm an atheist and I reject the whole idea of praying to a mystical god up in the sky because, frankly, it feels as fictional as D&D deities do to me. But I respect spiritual people and those who devote their lives to lifting up others through kindness and lending gentle support in their creative endeavors. I respect the caretakers, mental health providers, and counselors of the Material Plane for all they do simply to help out others. Dave is one of those people for me. I'm eternally grateful for his support in every conversation I have with him.

Crap, I think he's taking levels in cleric now too. I have to revise my earlier statement.

B. Dave Walters is the fighter/mage/thief/cleric of the D&D community.

That Time a Gnome Slapped
Joe Manganiello and Other Stories

On September 17, 2019, pro wrestler Maxwell Jacob Friedman (who goes by MJF in the ring) tweeted a photo of his beefy torso and proclaimed, "I don't play *Dungeons and Dragons*." Okay, dude. D&D isn't the same thing as eating carbs on a noncheat day. But we could all pick up what MJF was putting down. Or rather, who he was putting down. But fear not, underdogs. Shortly after that shot was fired, actor, director, writer, and epic-level D&D aficionado Joe Manganiello responded with a photo of his glistening, shirtless, ripped to Pelor torso from the cover of *Muscle & Fitness* and stated, "I do."

The internet went berserk, and we all got a big dose of bardic inspiration that day. Dungeon Masters, halflings, even Drizzt[1] himself could be found peeking from behind Joe's molded biceps, sneering and giving a big *nanner nanner foo foo*[2] at all the bullies, gym teachers, and misinformed parents who shunned *Dungeons & Dragons*. With just two words, Joe vindicated generations of kids who used to hide their rulebooks and endured insults and shame because of their nerdy hobby. Did Joe Manganiello single-handedly make D&D cool?

It's an odd day in the Wizards of the Coast offices when something happens that one might consider "strange." One time I wasn't paying attention and walked straight into a mind flayer's tentacle and dropped my lunch on the floor: not strange. On my first day, I had to help a Stormtrooper flummoxed

---

1. Shelly: Drizzt is the iconic drow created by best-selling author (and *Dragon Talk* friend!) R. A. Salvatore.
2. Shelly: That's draconic for F.U.

by how to print double-sided copies: not strange. I once walked past Nathan Stewart's office and saw Alcide Herveaux leaning over his desk,[3] geeking out over the cover art for an upcoming book. Okay, now *that* was strange.

"Uhh," I stammered. "I just emailed you that contract we were talking about."

"Cool, thanks!" Nathan answered, totally normal for a guy standing mere inches from someone named one of the sexiest men alive. Then, as if Nathan wasn't already being a total weirdo, he asked, "Do you know Joe?"

"Yeah," I said because, obviously I know Joe! You don't have to *know* Joe to know Joe. Then I ran into an empty conference room and texted all my friends.

"So this is strange . . ." I wrote.

Joe was visiting Wizards with his brother, Nick, fellow Carnegie Mellon alumni and playwright John Cassel, and his personal trainer, who happens to also be a CrossFit Games winner, Ron Mathews. Joe and Ron had been training together for years before their mutual love for D&D was discovered, and they've been playing together ever since. Being surrounded by tall, ridiculously fit, attractive guys geeking out about Dragonlance novels almost sounds like a *Saturday Night Live* skit, but I've seen it with my own blinded-by-the-dancing-lights eyes. You've come a long way, D&D.

Later that day, I had the chance to show Joe and John an early prototype of the *Betrayal at Baldur's Gate* board game. Halfway through, Joe turned into a minotaur and killed my character (definitely needed more playtesting).

It became less weird to see Joe around the office. He started Death Saves, a "fantasy-metal" streetwear clothing company and sold D&D T-shirts at our annual company meeting. He had sincere, earnest conversations with artists and designers about what he loves about D&D. He hosted weekly, star-studded game nights at his home. You spend a few minutes talking about elves and dragonborns with him and you'll forget he's married to Sofia Vergara.

I'm still not sure how we managed it, but Joe agreed to take time away from our much cooler coworkers to talk to Greg and me on *Dragon Talk*. Famous people don't really faze me thanks to my earlier career doing promotions for record labels. I chauffeured around, ran errands, and nearly had to buy illegal drugs for some of the early 1990s biggest alternative one-hit wonders. Joe didn't faze me because when he was around, he was genuinely interested in

3. Shelly: Alcide was Joe's beloved werewolf character from *True Blood*.

what we were working on and telling us about his latest campaign. It was like he forgot he was a celebrity.

Greg and I told Joe we were former theater majors to establish a peer-to-peer connection.

"You *were*?" Joe asked, rather incredulously.

Jeez man, it's not like I claimed to have gotten 1600 on my SATs. Clearly, he's never heard my C-3PO impression.

Joe's onramp to D&D started with—wait for it—*The Hobbit*, which he read in second grade. (Second grade?!) Joe's journey to Middle-earth led him to the D&D Red Box and hours playing through the solo adventure until he discovered AD&D with the neighbor kids. From there it was Endless Quest books and eventually the extensive Dragonlance library penned by Margaret Weis and Tracy Hickman. He took some time off because of things like college, girls, and honing his acting skills—the latter of which helped land him an iconic role on a hit TV show steeped in fantasy and beloved by the Comic Con crowd. Thanks to *True Blood*, Joe's love affair with D&D was rekindled. There must have been something in the water on that set because Joe's co-star, Deborah Ann Woll, was also busy spreading the good word of D&D with castmates and crew.

Surprising to no one (especially those of you who listen to *Dragon Talk*), Hollywood is full of past and present roleplayers. Joe confirmed lots of influential, prolific Hollywood producers and directors cut their teeth on tabletop gaming, which in turn developed their love for world building and storytelling. No big budgets are needed to bring your blockbuster to life around the gaming table. Low risk and high reward—it's the ultimate testing ground.

Joe's eventual descent into Dungeon Mastering started the same way the movie classic *Mystic Pizza* did—one idyllic summer in a New England town. In Joe's case, it was an island off the coast of Maine where his family spent summers. His aunt introduced him to a bunch of kids who happened to be on their way home from a comic bookstore. The memory was so clear in Joe's mind that he could still picture the cover of the Teenage Mutant Ninja Turtles comic they bought. These kids were avid roleplayers who welcomed Joe into their fold. He started Dungeon Mastering a homebrew world and pretty much hasn't stopped.

"It was like the *Island of Misfit Toys*," Joe said.

Yes, Joe, a cowboy who rides an ostrich, a train with square wheels, and a future dragonborn oathbreaker were all banished to an island because who could possibly love this crew?

You might be familiar with Arkhan (a.k.a. Arkhan the Cruel), Joe's iconic dragonborn paladin. During one of Joe's visits to Wizards, he pitched and later wrote an outline involving the Hand of Vecna,[4] Tiamat, and an epic backstory for Arkhan that was published in the official D&D adventure *Baldur's Gate: Descent into Avernus*.[5] Arkhan dabbled in necromancy (with his zombie minions) and worshipped Tiamat (as one does) and can be found depicted on T-shirts, pendants, and even miniatures. He was lawful good until 3rd level, when it was time to make his oath. Then all hell broke loose and things went, well, south for our dragonborn friend. A typical Friday night for Arkhan might involve torching a room full of sleeping goblins and "never feeling more alive." The goblins couldn't say the same.

Joe recounted a story that's one of the best in-game moments I've ever heard. There was a button-pushing gnome who, according to Joe, made him "lose his mind." After Arkhan had enough, he grabbed the gnome by the scruff of his neck, hoisted him to eye level, and was about to let loose. But he failed his Intimidation check. Unfazed by Joe, the gnome hauled off and slapped Arkhan across the face. It was all just so perfect. The Dungeon Master who created this seemingly innocuous NPC, Joe's visceral response to him, the gnome's delusion of grandeur, and the dice conspiring to make what could have been just a small exchange turn into one of those moments you talk about for years. Arkhan retaliated by burning down the gnome's bar, smashing his inventory, and surrounding him with a good old-fashioned *hellish rebuke*.[6]

Joe mentioned how he was still trying to explain D&D to Sofia. She got the overall concept, but sometimes asked, "Who won?" Once when Nathan was heading to L.A. to meet with Joe, I gave him a copy of *Confessions of a Part-Time Sorceress* in hopes it would make its way to Sofia. She was my target audience, after all. Nathan said he made the drop but saw it in the same spot on the kitchen counter the next day.

Greg and I managed what I like to call a "solid interview." But we could only

4. Shelly: The Hand of Vecna is one of the most bizarre and iconic magic items of all time. Lopping off your own hand and reattaching this ol' lich's severed hand granted the wearer super strength, magical powers, and a penchant toward evil-doings. Oh, and if the hand was ever removed, the wearer would be killed.

5. Shelly: Joe has been involved in other D&D projects, but they haven't been announced yet and I really like my job, so you'll just have to wait and see.

6. Greg: This D&D fifth edition spell is the equivalent of a fire-tinged "Bitch, please!" you can only cast after your character is hit with an attack.

play it cool for so long. After the interview, Greg asked Joe to record a happy birthday message for his wife, and I asked for a photo in a way I hoped made it sound like standard interview procedure. He graciously agreed to both requests and after wishing Erin a very happy birthday, he inserted his towering figure between Greg and me. One thundering arm went around Greg's shoulders, and I braced for impact as his left arm crept toward me. Praise Tymora, please don't let me pass out. I was inches from nestling into Joe's magnificent armpit when I caught sight of a beautiful bicep out of the corner of my eye making an upward motion. "It's coming for meeeeeeeeee," I thought. But alas, his arm nearest my shoulders remained vertical while the beautifully hand-carved wood ampersand we used as set decor got a nice little cuddle.

Talk about a slap in the face. Cool picture though.

shelly

The Journey Continues

An unexpected thing happened recently. Kari, mother of the *Last Airbender*–loving kids, told me her daughters have been asking questions about D&D.

Earlier in the school year, I dropped off copies of the *Young Adventurer's Guides* by Jim Zub and Stacy King for Quinn's classroom, and he said they basically caused a riot. There were only eight books, and twenty-five kids all wanted to read them. The poor teacher had to resort to drawing names out of a hat to decide who could borrow them first. Apparently, the words "Dungeons" and "Dragons" are very enticing to third-graders.

"What kind of questions?" I asked Kari, imagining my friend having to field inquiries like "Mommy, how do I ready an action?" Or "What are the spell components needed to cast *Raulothim's psychic damage*?"

She lowered her voice and looked around. "They wanted to know if I knew how to play."

"Wow," I said, "Parenting books just don't talk about this moment. What did you tell them?"

"I said no, but we knew two people who did."

Naturally my first instinct was to be miffed at my friend for putting me in this uncomfortable situation! Telling people I know how to play *Dungeons & Dragons*? Just because I happened to work for the game's publisher for two decades and change? Come on! They knew one person—Bart! Do not come to me for your learnings and curiosities about this game! I only know how to play low-level magic users, and most of my party members would seriously question the use of the word "know." Nope! Not meeeeee!

But before I could begin that speech, Kari put her hands on my shoulders, looked me straight in the eyes, and with more sincerity than Grandpa Joe from *Charlie and the Chocolate Factory* said, "My daughters want to play *Dungeons & Dragons*."

I was not prepared for how I would respond to that.

I froze. It could have been hours I stood there on the sidewalk in front of our recycling bin and Little Free Library stuffed with D&D stickers and the occasional d20. A puffiness rose in my chest and a lump in my throat. Finally, I found the words.

"Then they must learn," I said. "I will teach them."

Was this what Batman felt every time the Bat-Signal appeared? Here we had nine-year-old girls wanting to play *Dungeons & Dragons*. Isn't this the very reason I go to work every day? Isn't this kind of my job description? Isn't this the greatest thing ever? These are the stories Greg and I get all weepy over! I had a chance to be part of someone's story. Yes, these girls needed *Dungeons & Dragons*, but more importantly, *Dungeons & Dragons* needed them.

How could I deny the youth of today? It was my civic duty.

The following Sunday, I drank nineteen cups of coffee, pulled the *D&D Essentials Kit* out of the garage, read a few paragraphs from the adventure, and called it good. This was nothing like the weeks of prep I did years ago. These kids didn't know the rules, so they wouldn't know if I messed up. Besides, I had candy. Lots and lots of candy in case things started to go sideways (that's good advice for all new DMs). I had Bart lined up to co-DM and told him he had to be the cleric. I'm a mom first and Dungeon Master second. No way was I sending these children into the wilds without a healer. A few hours later, the girls and my son took their seats at our kitchen table.

"*Dungeons & Dragons* is a collaborative storytelling game," I told them. "That means we're going to work together to tell a story and have an amazing adventure!"

They were hooked.

I did it! I was a Dungeon Master! Turns out, I did know how to make a skill check, read a stat block, and improvise when I had no idea where the story was going. I can even do voices other than Bert from *Sesame Street* and C-3PO. I stood on the shoulders of every "How to DM" guest and heard their soothing words of advice roll through my subconscious.

"Give them something familiar to latch on to!"

"Give them an opportunity to feel powerful."

"Give them more candy!"

It was in me all along. And it was magic, baby.

I had many revelations after our first game:

1. Dungeon Mastering is really fun.
2. Rules, schmules. Go with whatever makes the story better.
3. If I can do it, anyone can do it.
4. My son cast spells out of his butt, and honestly, I'm kind of here for it.
5. Teaching kids how to play D&D may be my purpose in life.

After they went home, I spent the rest of the day feeling like a director on preview night waiting for the reviews to come in the next day. What if they hated it? What if I ruined their impression of D&D forever? What if Kari was mad at how much sugar I let her kids have? The next day Kari found me at school drop-off. The reviews were in! The girls couldn't stop talking about it—the goblins that tried to lure them off the path with poisoned milk and cookies, the dwarves they had to warn about the threat of a dragon attack, the ooze Megan attacked that ended up splitting into two ooze monsters! They quoted funny lines from NPCs and retold inside jokes. They were so proud of how Maya convinced their school principal (and quest giver) to give them nearly twice the reward for completing a successful mission. They laughed about ditching Chunky Cheese (Quinn's wizard) in the forest and taking his share of the loot (you gotta admire that move). They loved all of it. Even Kari thanked me. Her daughters are typically shy and reserved, but they were bursting with a newfound energy and excitement. They came alive at the table, totally embodying their characters and embracing the spirit of make-believe. Even Quinn said he couldn't believe how talkative they were— or that they left him alone in the woods.

We played a second time, with their six-year-old brother and Kari, because they literally begged me to. I have a sneaking suspicion there will be other sessions. Chunky Cheese might hang out in the woods a bit longer because I'm thinking of inviting a few other neighborhood girls and their moms to join our party.

There was one more important revelation: anyone can play D&D. Even people who don't think of themselves as roleplayers or fantasy fans. Kids, adults, Midwest mothers, and middle-school girls. Therapists, scientists, theater majors, and politicians. Introverts, extroverts, teachers, actors, and athletes.

Even fans of the *Real Housewives*. You're never too young for your first quest or too old to cast your first *magic missile*.

As Whitney Houston once said, "I believe the children are our future. Teach them how to play D&D and let them lead the way!" Maybe not those exact words, but I'm pretty sure that was the sentiment. After five decades, *Dungeons & Dragons* still captivates the hearts and minds of those who play. I can't help but imagine a new generation of nine-year-old kids laying eyes on the *Monster Manual* for the first time and all the creativity that will unlock. Who knows? Maybe in twenty years they'll be guests on *Dragon Talk*. When asked about their origin story, they'll say something like, "Our friend's mom taught us! We got slimed by an ooze monster, nearly fell off a half-tamed manticore midflight, ditched her weirdo son who cast *ray of frost* out of his butt, and split his share of the reward. She was the coolest person ever!" (It's my fantasy, okay?)

One year while Greg was neck deep in D&D Live planning, a *Dragon Talk* guest commented on how much work coordinating an event like that must be. It was, Greg admitted, but it didn't feel like work. We're making games, having fun, and as a bonus, listening to people tell us how meaningful playing D&D has been to them. I think about that conversation all the time. Collectively our jobs are to get people excited for *Dungeons & Dragons* and make sure everyone who is curious about it, has always wanted to play, or maybe hasn't discovered it yet can find their way to a table. It's work, but it's not hard work. Pull up a chair. This party is just getting started.

greg

Your Next Adventure

Hopefully after reading this book, you are inspired to jump into the D&D community and start playing (if you aren't already). In many ways, that's what this book, this podcast, and our continued employment at Wizards of the Coast is all about! *Dragon Talk* leads by example, showing that you don't have to be super knowledgeable about all the history or lore—you don't even have to really know the rules—to enjoy the storytelling framework D&D provides. Experience at playing pretend when you were (or are) a kid is all the prerequisite you really need.

But to offer some concrete ways to get in the game, I wanted to give you a few things you can do to start rolling dice with your friends. I'm presenting these in no particular order. Try one or all of these if they fit within your habits or lifestyle.

Watch introductory or instructional videos online. YouTube and Twitch are wonderful sources for information that show how easy it is to start playing D&D. Search "How to Start D&D" on YouTube, and you'll find tons of creators who have demystified this game for their audiences. Pick one or two and stick with the creator who most speaks to you.

Watch or listen to people who play D&D. As I said in the introduction, this is perhaps the secret sauce for D&D's boom in popularity the past few years because showing works so much better than telling. There are too many creators to list here, but *Acquisitions Incorporated*, *Critical Role*, and *Dimension 20* are some marquee entertainment properties to start with to see how D&D is played. It's important to note that those are produced by professional actors with production budgets, so it won't be what your first game will be like. You may find it more fun to look at smaller creators who are telling a story that fits your style, and there are plenty to choose from out there. Podcasts can be illustrative too, and you can listen while working out or commuting so you don't have to feel like you must sit in front of a screen to learn how to play.

Just start playing D&D. Sometimes the best way to get into any hobby is to just try it and learn as you go. Starting as a player is generally encouraged, so an experienced DM can ease you into the process. Head to your local game store, if there's one nearby, and ask the employees if there's a group looking for new players. Gaming conventions often have new-player-friendly games too. If playing online sounds like less of a hurdle than meeting new people in person, check out the D&D Discord channel to look for groups or sign up for the programs D&D runs called Adventurers League. Adventurers League is designed for both new and experienced players to play two-hour sessions of a D&D story that highlights all aspects of the game.

Dungeon Master for your group/family. A trimmed-down version of the D&D rules you need to play is available for free from the Dungeonsand dragons.com website. That's a great way to familiarize yourself with how the rules work if you have experience reading board game instructions. (Note: If putting together IKEA furniture is tough for you, that may not be the best option.) Picking up the *D&D Essentials Kit* or a *D&D Starter Set* is another option—these kits have everything you need to start playing, including dice, maps, and easier to understand rules.

Whichever way you go about starting to play D&D, don't fret about getting everything exactly right the first time—you won't! Like riding a bike, crocheting a hat, or putting together a puzzle, playing D&D gets easier each time you play until—click!—it all falls into place. Have fun, tell fantastic stories, and may your dice rolls always be twenties.

Who knows? Maybe we'll have you on the podcast one day soon.

ACKNOWLEDGMENTS

We extend endless gratitude to all the generous guests who have graced *Dragon Talk* to share their passion, creativity, talent, and origin story with us. You truly lift us up every day, and we are so lucky to know you. Without the *Dragon Talk* listeners, we'd be making potty jokes into the void, so thank you to everyone who has given our podcast a listen, a like, subscribed, and took the time to write a review begging us not to sing anymore. We hear you but cannot make any promises.

Thank you to Ryan Marth and Lisa Carr of Siren Sound. Ryan, we still think you're too good for us, but we love you and your passion for "good, clean audio" so much. Please don't forget us when your film career takes off. Lisa, you make us look good. Thank you for taking it up 729 notches. We would be lost without you. Thanks to Pelham Greene for the early days and sounding the air horn, Bart Carroll for getting this whole thing started, and Sean Mayovsky for the production help and always knowing which cord goes to what piece of equipment.

Much gratitude to Wizards of the Coast, the fine people who gave us their blessing to write this book: Liz Schuh, Brian Perry, Ray Winninger, and Nathan Stewart. Also for our day jobs.

Thanks to Tanya DePass and Rico Corazón for reading *Welcome to Dragon Talk* and letting us know if our silly jokes make sense to everyone. Greg still misses that *Perfect Strangers* reference, but it was for the best to cut it.

Thank you to the University of Iowa Press and especially our very patient editor, Meredith Stabel, for sending Shelly the greatest email ever and giving us this opportunity! You are a joy to work with, even though Shelly doesn't understand comma use and Greg never met a footnote he didn't love. Thank you, Tegan Daly for all you do behind the scenes. And thank you, Laura Poole, for cleaning everything up and making us look better. We hope you join your friends and start playing D&D!

Shelly: I also want to thank Bart Carroll (again) because I didn't dedicate this book to him and feel a tiny bit bad. Thank you, Quinn, my funny, charming, big-hearted child. You may look like your dad, but everyone knows that "spells coming out of your butt" is all me. Endless gratitude to Chris Lindsay and Chris Tulach because they not only tolerated but very thoughtfully answered all my inane D&D rules and lore questions. A nod to my dad, Tom Mazzanoble, because he'll think it's cool to see his name in a book. Huge thank you to Megan and Maya Murphy for rewarding me with inspiration and unlocking a passion I never knew I had. I hope you never lose your sense of adventure. Thank you to all the kids—past, present, and future—who lost and found themselves in D&D and have (or will) grown up to be kind, empathetic, generous, and creative leaders. The world will be better because of you. Finally, thank you to Saritza Hernandez—champion for all things geeky. I can't believe I found an agent who plays D&D! We've only just begun.

Greg: Thanks to Nathan Stewart for taking a chance and hiring me at Wizards of the Coast. This book and the podcast wouldn't exist without him! I am eternally grateful to my wife, Erin, for joining me in this long, strange adventure across the country and for letting me stay up at night to write this book (and maybe play a few games). I would also like to thank the Brandon Collection, a box of hand-me-downs my parents obtained from a neighbor in the 1980s that included flannel shirts, torn jeans, and a copy of the *Dungeon Master's Guide*. My interest in D&D wouldn't have existed without finding that book on my older brothers' shelf. Finally, thank you to my brother Mario for showing me the animated film *The Hobbit* when I was five, telling me events that were in the book, and sparking the love of fantasy storytelling that drives my creativity to this day. I'm ready to tell more stories!